The Young and the Restless

Most Memorable Moments

The Young and the Restless

Most Memorable Moments

MARY CASSATA AND BARBARA IRWIN

General Publishing Group Los Angeles

Publisher: W. Quay Hays
Editor: Peter Hoffman
Art Director: Susan Anson
Production Director: Trudihope Schlomowitz
Color and Pre-Press Manager: Bill Castillo
Production Artist: Gaston Moraga
Production Assistants: David Chadderdon, Tom Archibeque, Phillis Stacy, Lisa Barnes, Gus Dawson
Copyeditor: Steve Baeck

The Publisher wishes to thank Lee Phillip Bell, Bill Bell, Lucy Johnson, Nancy Wiard
and Harriet Robinson for their kind contributions to this book.

For information:
General Publishing Group, Inc.
2701 Ocean Park Boulevard
Santa Monica, CA 90405

Library of Congress Cataloging-in-Publication Data

Cassata, Mary B.
    The young and the restless : most memorable moments / by Mary Cassata and Barbara Irwin.
        p.   cm.
    ISBN 1-881649-87-3
    1. Young and the restless (Television program)   I. Irwin, Barbara.   II. Title.
    PN1992.77.Y635C37   1996
    791.45'72—dc20   96-36400
                                                                                            CIP

Printed in the USA by RR Donnelley & Sons Company
10 9 8 7 6 5 4 3 2 1

General Publishing Group
Los Angeles

Table of Contents

Preface

The working title had been "The Innocent Years!," until Lee and I came to an inescapable conclusion when we were creating the show in 1972. We were confronted with the very disturbing reality that young America had lost much of its innocence. Innocence as we had known and lived it all our lives had, in so many respects, ceased to exist. We needed another title, one that reflected the youth and mood of the early seventies. Thus was born "The Young and the Restless"!

From its concept, the force and focus of "Y & R" was its younger characters. The fabulous Foster family: older son Snapper, laconic, introspective, soon to start his internship; Greg, vital, outgoing, personable, a recent graduate of Yale Law School; Jill, 17, foregoing school, employed as a beautician; and Liz, a single parent whose husband had deserted the family years ago—a tough mother because she had to be, and the glue that kept this family together.

Then there was the Brooks family. Newspaper publisher Stuart and his wife Jennifer were the parents of four very different, yet contemporary young women. Beautiful Chris, 18, in love with love; Leslie, the oldest, introverted though very talented, her goal to become a concert pianist; Lorie, very much a free spirit and part of the youth movement while a student in Paris; and, finally, Peggy, 16, disarmingly and refreshingly uncomplicated in a time that was becoming more and more complex.

There was Sally, the waitress at Pierre's, who loved Snapper but had to settle for a "no strings" relationship. And Kay Chancellor, a rich, desperately unhappy alcoholic—played by the incomparable Jeanne Cooper, who brought enormous impact to her role and to the show. In the early years, we brought two unknown actors—Tom Selleck and David Hasselhoff—into our company. Today they are both major stars.

We later brought a man onto the show for a short-term role, several months at the most, very probably less. This remarkable actor is still with us to this day; the death which was to be part of his story instantly changed after we saw his first performance. That man, if you haven't already guessed, is Eric Braeden, who plays Victor Newman. Eric arrived perhaps a year after Melody Thomas. What wonderful stories and moments these two have brought to "Y & R" since then!

Bill and Lee Bell

As time went on it became necessary to make adjustments, major adjustments. Within a few months, the Brooks and Foster families gave way to the Abbotts: Jack, Ashley, Traci and John; and the Williamses: Paul, Patty, Steve, Mary and Carl. Through the years we have added scores of characters who have greatly impacted the show, most recently Hope. This lovable, sightless woman affected so many lives, especially Victor's. And there was our very warm and wonderful Asian family, personified by the beautiful and talented Elizabeth Sung, who portrayed Luan. One of our most powerful stories ever occurred during the past several years, involving Drucilla and Neil, Olivia and Nathan, Malcolm and Keesha and young Nate Jr.

About 13 years ago three characters joined "Y & R," two of whom are with us to this day. The other has been with our sister show, "The Bold and the Beautiful" for almost eight years. Remember Rose DeVille, and, of course, those two young kids, Nina Webster and Cricket Blair, and the black market baby story? Nina still hasn't found her baby, though we suspect someday that might very well happen. And Cricket with her various love affairs—her first love, Phillip Chancellor III; then Danny Romalotti, who treated her like a little sister for many years only to awaken to the reality that this young lady was now a woman; and more recently Paul Williams is in the forefront of her life.

In closing, we thank you for your friendship and loyalty. We hope you enjoy reliving these memorable moments and trust the best is yet to come.

—Lee and Bill Bell

Introduction

Edward Scott

How does one describe the experience of working on a Bill Bell show? The first word that comes to my mind is intense—beginning with a dynamic, creative genius with imaginative and innovative storytelling powers that know no equal, compelling characters and relationships, rich dialogue, and a message that entertains and informs millions around the world. My challenge has been to take it from the page to the stage, to make it all work and make it work well. Kudos and crises, fun and agony, laughter and tears (along with some pretty salty language)—20 terrific years working with a creative force that has no equal on television.

Behind that force lies the seasoned and experienced producing talent to pull it off: Kay Alden, our co-head writer who has been with us for over two decades, our gifted writing staff, an outstanding directing team, a unique acting company with unsurpassed depth and range and a veteran production and administrative team. They all arrive for work every day eager to contribute their gifts and talents. It's an awesome and humbling responsibility to hold the reins.

Another different challenge is to work on a show with a social conscience—how to entertain and inform at the same time, while raising consciousness on some very contemporary issues. Bill Bell knows how to write about an issue and to subtly build a story around it, using ongoing characters and storylines the audience is already committed to, and then grabbing the interest of the audience with key dramatic incidents. The first mastectomy on television, crack babies, illiteracy, cults, depression, bulimia and eating disorders, teen pregnancies, a face-lift actually performed on camera, infant CPR, sexual harassment, date rape, black-market adoption, antismoking campaigns, euthanasia, the homeless, runaways, a "Save the Earth" environmental theme, the first rock 'n' roll concerts on daytime, the list goes on. Their impact has been enormous.

Fascinating characters all come together to entice, enfold, and entertain in compelling stories, all bathed in the "Y&R" look that, since episode one, has set the industry standard for direction, lighting and sound, music, set decoration, wardrobe and editing.

You, our audience, always have our commitment, respect and appreciation. To paraphrase Noel Coward and describe our philosophy: "Always leave the audience begging for more. Never, ever bore the living hell out of it."

—*Edward Scott*

Acknowledgments

Our experiences in compiling the information and writing the moments for this book have been among the most memorable of our careers. We owe a debt of gratitude to many.

Most importantly, to Bill Bell and his partner, Lee, for selecting us to write this book in the first place, and for guiding us and helping to achieve its final form.

And to the incomparable Nancy Bradley Wiard, coordinating producer, for the numerous smooth trails she blazed for us, and for sharing her treasure trove of knowledge.

To Kay Alden for putting up with our many interruptions to answer the numerous questions we asked of her.

To Lucy Johnson, Senior Vice President of Daytime/ Children's Programs and Special Projects at CBS, for inspiring us and setting us on course as the project began.

To Andrea Joel for her generous and enthusiastic spirit in providing us with archival materials, enhancing these pages beyond our wildest dreams.

To the CBS Photo Department in Los Angeles, which became our second home for many weeks, for making us feel we were one of them by opening not only their doors but their hearts—notably, Francis Cavanaugh, Kathleen Tanji, Rouhi Taylor and Judy Margolin.

Our thanks go to Catherine Bitran of SONY Signatures, who was one of our first contacts, paving the way for us to work with General Publishing Group, and to Jack Westerkamp, who followed the project through to its completion. To Ed Zimmerman of Columbia Tristar Television for sharing his expertise and archival materials with us, and to Malka Youngstein for giving us access to the Columbia Tristar International Television photo archives.

To *Soap Opera Digest*, especially Jody Reines, *Soap Opera Weekly,* and *Soap Opera Now*, for being invaluable resources in our research. And to Robert Christie of the National Academy of Television Arts and Sciences for helping us locate Emmy photos.

Frank Tobin and Charles Sherman of Frank Tobin Public Relations couldn't have been more responsive in arranging interviews and filling our many requests for information, which they did freely and promptly.

To Brigitte Kueppers and the staff at the UCLA Film and Television Library for giving us "special" access to the William J. Bell Collection.

To Executive Producer Edward Scott and Producer David Shaughnessy for sharing their accounts of the challenges in producing Y&R and for treating us as one of the crew.

To the following actors who shared their most memorable moments with us: Marla Adams, Lauralee Bell, Peter Bergman, Eric Braeden, Jeanne Cooper, Doug Davidson, Jerry Douglas, Sharon Farrell, Kate Linder, Shemar Moore, Joshua Morrow, Victoria Rowell, Kristoff St. John, Melody Thomas Scott, Jess Walton, Tonya Lee Williams and William Wintersole.

To the behind-the-scenes staff at Y&R who gave us their time, notably Scott Anderson, Joe Bevacqua, Gail Camacho, Fred Cooper, Patti Denney, Jez Davidson Guito, James Houghton, William Hultstrom, Jennifer Johns, Jill Newton, Kathi Nishimoto and Barry Wittman. To Eva Arquero, Debbie Catanese, Josh O'Connell and Nora Wade for helping manage the long-distance details.

To the staff of General Publishing Group: Quay Hays for his faith in us; Susan Anson for her spectacular design work; our editor Peter Hoffman with whom we shared the many moments of anguish and exhilaration it took to bring this book to life; and to Sharon Hays and Harlan Boll, who were there to enlighten and guide us.

To our friends and colleagues in the Communication Departments at the State University of New York at Buffalo and Canisius College, and to Terry Fisher and David Lesinski of the Canisius College Media Center for their incredible support.

To Randolph J. Granat and Lawrence Felckowski, who spent long hours looking up materials and manning the photocopy machine, to Al and to Drs. Barbara Martin and Sylvia Regalla who were there for us.

Finally, we are forever indebted to our families for understanding when we put the rest of our lives on hold to meet deadlines, for inspiration and support and for remaining steadfast: James Klein, Frances Irwin, Doris Lueth, William Irwin, Michele and Ken Klein, Magic and Hanchy, Jennifer and Sal Ballachino, Alvira, Fred, Sharon and Dominic Cassata, Sally Collopy and most of all, Mama and Sam.

The Moment When It All Began

A lone semi made its way along the interstate. Next stop: Genoa City. The passenger on board was a mystery man, Chicago doctor Brad Eliot. He'd been mugged and left for dead while trying to escape a past he chose to forget. Genoa City was as good a place as any to start a new life.

Across town, medical student Snapper Foster lent a sympathetic ear to his friend, waitress Sally McGuire:

SALLY: (MORE TO HERSELF)

Kind of a drag, isn't it. Stuck in a place like

Genoa City.

                 (BEAT)

God, I feel so restless.

            (AS WE DISSOLVE TO...)

        MUSIC UP TO FINISH AND OUT

            FADE TO: BLACK

            UP ON: FILM LOGO

the
YOUNG
and the
RESTLESS

*O*n March 26, 1973, "The Young and The Restless" made its debut on CBS, and daytime television would never be the same again. It was the soap opera that revolutionized the genre. It had a style all its own. The focus? In the words of its creators, chemistry. Man-woman chemistry. And involvement—it drew the viewer in with strong, empathic characters played by breathtakingly beautiful actors. Characters to whom viewers could relate. Characters they would learn to love and love to hate. Socially conscious story lines. Storylines that entertained, but at the same time enlightened. And music. In the background and in the spotlight.

Twenty-three years later, "The Young and the Restless" is still going strong. Stronger than ever. It's a show characterized by quality. Consistency. Continuity. Integrity. The vision of a single person. That person is William J. Bell. He and his wife, Lee Phillip Bell, cocreated "The Young and the Restless," and continue at the helm to this day. Over the years, many memorable moments, big and small—far too many to recount them all—have graced the television screens of Y&R's viewers.

The big moments. Moments that pack a punch. The lowest of lows balanced with the highest of highs. Great love stories, and great deceptions. Intriguing mysteries and down and dirty crimes. Major productions that burst off the television screen, taking viewers on fantastic voyages to fantasylands. Memorable couples and memorable triangles. Complex, multidimensional characters, some memorable for the dastardly deeds they've done, and others memorable because they're genuinely good people. Characters anchored in memorable families.

And then there are the small moments, more a part of the everyday world in which we live. The day-to-day moments. The cadence of a character's speech, a certain look or glance, the reaction or lack of reaction, the smile, the frown, the gleam, the handshake, the touch. The everyday kinds of truths. All of these moments, big and small, add up to the memories that sustain us.

"The Young and the Restless" began its momentous journey in Genoa City on that memorable Monday in 1973, and instantly and forever changed the face of daytime television.

Love and Romance

Hooray for love! Love is a carousel which we all hope to ride at one time or another, or two or three. Love makes some of us happy and others sad, some of us good and others bad. Love can be the balm of a sweet-sounding violin or the afterburst of an awesome holocaust. It's the stimulant for the young that makes them feel restless and the chamomile tea for the not so young that makes them feel rested. Love is what makes life worth living, if only for a fleeting moment or for a moment that lasts beyond the grave. Many of the lovers on "The Young and the Restless" vowed to relinquish their restlessness by saying "I do."

The Greatest Love Stories

*A*lthough not all soap opera couples who marry manage to stay together, in some unions there remains a link that forever binds man and woman together no matter what the fates decree. Throughout the history of "The Young and the Restless," four couples have remained inextricably bound together, if not in the physical sense then in their minds and souls. The reel-ality was that Chris Brooks understood love before Snapper did; and Nikki stripped away all doubts before Victor did; Cricket and Danny learned they could not wrap their love in a dreamcoat; and Jack and Luan were separated by half a world before they found their love again.

SNAPPER AND CHRIS:
Now and Forever

Idealistic college student Chris Brooks, whose family was comfortably well-off, had eyes only for poor, struggling medical student, Snapper (William) Foster. Snapper, too, was smitten, and though the couple had open and frank conversations about sex, Chris could not bring herself to Snapper's bed before marriage. When Chris was raped and retreated from all social contact, Snapper was instantly at her side, gently but firmly leading her back to the world of the living. The two lovers married, with Snapper patiently waiting for Chris to be emotionally ready to consummate their marriage. Their union has remained strong, and today the couple resides in London, where Snapper continues to practice medicine.

The vows Snapper said to Chris, which she, in turn, repeated to him:

> I join you in marriage, Chris, to be my wife now and forever. To hold and keep you, in joy and sorrow, prosperity and hardship, health and sickness, to honor and defend you, to love and cherish, and together keep holy the word of God.

Snapper slipped Chris's wedding band on her finger while his brother, Greg, looked on.

Before the wedding ceremony began, Chris, with her mother, Jennifer, at her side, looked approvingly at her wedding party: (left to right) Lorie, Leslie, Peggy and Stuart, with future sister-in-law Jill in the background.

The happy bride and groom were among the first of "The Young and the Restless" couples to be married in Genoa City.

NIKKI AND VICTOR:
Through the Eyes of Love

Victor proposed to Nikki from his hospital bed, where he was recovering from the harpoon wounds inflicted upon him by Rick Daros as he was trying to rescue his beloved. She wanted to marry him immediately, but Victor retracted his proposal after hearing from his doctor that his wounds may have made him impotent. Deciding it would be best to leave Genoa City and to keep his distance from Nikki, Victor asked Douglas to drive him to the airport. On the way, Victor occupied himself by looking at sensuous photographs Douglas had given him of his beloved, stripping. Within moments, Victor ordered Douglas to turn the car around. "Return me to Nikki," he said. "I don't believe I have a problem anymore."

Their wedding day was magical: The glow on Nikki's face, the unmistakable pride in Victor's eyes as he beheld his beautiful bride and Gina Roma's sensuous rendition of "Through the Eyes of Love." No expense had been spared to make this spellbinding, lush extravaganza worthy of the bride of Victor Newman. Nikki's gown, the creation of one of L.A.'s top fashion houses, used 70 yards of imported French silk-faced satin and organza, and took the talent and wizardry of more than a dozen seamstresses 500 hours to produce. The dress, its 10-foot train and the royal crown were all hand-beaded with over 20,000 small beads and pearls. On the guest list were many of Nikki's and Victor's family and friends from earlier years (Chris, Leslie and Peggy Brooks, Derek Thurston, Brock Reynolds, Casey Reed, and Maestro Fausch) as well as an assemblage of oil barons, Arab sheiks and Japanese businessmen. It was a fairy-tale wedding which made the mind, heart and spirit soar.

Victor's friend and confidant, Douglas Austin, knew what was good for Victor and grabbed a photo album of Nikki stripping to remind Victor of old times.

Dr. Casey Reed assisted her sister, the happy bride-to-be, before the ceremony.

Victor Newman
and
Nikki Reed
invite you to share their joy
as they celebrate their marriage
at
The Colonnade Room
on Saturday, the seventeenth of July
nineteen hundred and eighty-four
at five-thirty o'clock

No expense was spared to showcase the bride of powerful Victor Newman, who impishly sported polka dot boxer shorts underneath her gown.

Victor and his
bride exchanged
wedding vows.

John Abbott chatted with Kay Chancellor, whose long relationship with Nikki has been that of surrogate mother and true friend.

A veritable who's who of royalty and power were among the wedding guests.

Nikki and Victor Newman shared their first kiss as husband and wife.

CRICKET AND DANNY:
Starting Here, Starting Now

She was a teenage model. He was a budding rock star. Cricket and Danny grew up together, and even though they each had their share of relationships, they were always the best of friends. What started as a high school girl's crush blossomed into the deepest of loves. They were always there for each other, no matter what. When Danny proposed, Cricket, like every young woman in love, looked forward to her wedding to the man of her dreams. No setting could have been more fitting for the joining of their hearts than the idyllic paradise of the Hawaiian Islands.

The producers searched to find the perfect spot for Cricket and Danny's wedding: The Kaewalai church on the island of Maui. The gazebo was built especially for the ceremony.

As they grew up, Cricket and Danny were always the best of friends.

Cricket's half brother, Scott Grainger, gave her away.

Danny whisked Cricket away to get married; the guest list was small.
Nina stood up for her best friend. Danny's father, Rex, was best man.
His sister, Gina, serenaded them with "Starting Here, Starting Now"
during the ceremony.

Cricket and Danny posed for their first photo as husband and wife.

Danny and Cricket enjoyed a romantic honeymoon basking in the sun. With a history of bad weather on location shoots, Coordinating Producer Nancy Wiard arranged for the Hawaiian shoot to be blessed by a kahuna (Hawaiian priest). The weather couldn't have been better!

Luan toiled in the Saigon Shack restaurant, unaware that her love, Jack, was also in Genoa City.

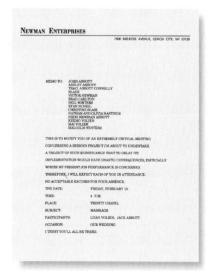

JACK AND LUAN:
A World Apart

They met under the worst of circumstances, but Jack and Luan discovered a love strong enough to transcend all the boundaries of culture, time and distance that separated them. As a 19-year-old American GI in Vietnam, Jack Abbott met the love of his life, but the fates stepped in and the lovers lost all contact. Unknown to Jack, Luan had become pregnant. Luan left her son, Keemo, behind and came to the States in search of her love. Just when it seemed like she would never find Jack, her prayers were answered. No other love is like a first love, and all their long-forgotten feelings came rushing back when they were finally reunited. All too soon after their marriage, Luan was taken again from Jack, but even in death, their love lives on.

Jack and Luan's wedding had the flavor of a traditional Vietnamese ceremony.

Luan, Jack, her daughter, Mai and their son, Keemo, were reunited after years of separation.

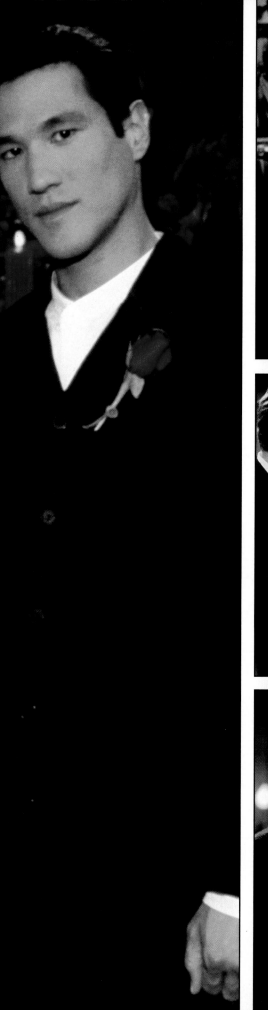

Above: Keemo greeted his friend Christine at the chapel. After Luan had been shot in a holdup, Paul and Christine had located Keemo and brought him back to Genoa City, giving Luan the will to live.

Left: They came from two different worlds, but a miracle brought Jack and Luan back together again.

Bottom: Jack would again lose Luan, this time to a fatal illness shortly after they were married.

Young Love

Nina and Phillip celebrated their marriage with best friends Cricket and Danny.

*S*ometimes it's the rush of a first love that sweeps them away and sometimes it's the need to defy one's family to pursue a forbidden love. It could be as simple as hormones raging out of control. Young love takes many forms. One thing remains the same—at least one, and often both, of the young lovers find themselves on the threshold of adulthood. But rather than dealing with the mundane problems of most high school kids, they're often leaping over hurdles that make them grow up very quickly. "The Young and the Restless" has had its share of young lovers who've made it to the altar.

NINA AND PHILLIP:
His Fair Lady

Nina Webster: teenage unwed mother, greedy and crafty beyond her years, more than a little rough around the edges. Phillip Chancellor III: shy, kind, sensitive, heir to the Chancellor family fortune. No one, least of all Phillip—who was dating Nina's best friend Cricket—could ever see them as a couple. When Nina took advan-

Phillip Chancellor, himself a product of a broken home, didn't want his son to grow up with the same heartache.

tage of Phillip after he had been drinking and she wound up pregnant, Phillip was furious. He hated her for it, but he hated himself even more. Putting her own feelings aside, Cricket encouraged Phillip to spend time with Nina, and, more importantly, with his son, while Nina, with coaching from Danny and Cricket, underwent an amazing transformation and became a fitting bride for the young Mr. Chancellor. The couple was genuinely in love, but unfortunately their marriage was to be short-lived. Phillip was tragically killed in an automobile accident.

VICTORIA AND RYAN:
Young Love, Forbidden Love

Sixteen-year-old Victoria Newman turned to Ryan McNeil for comfort when she saw her parents drifting farther apart. And even though one night with Ryan was enough to convince Victoria she wasn't ready for sexual intimacy, she didn't want to give him up. Ever the opportunist, Ryan saw Vicki as the key to his own quick climb up the corporate ladder at Newman Enterprises. He gave her an engagement ring, but she decided they shouldn't go public with their news. Upset that they were seeing each other, Victor tried to pay Ryan off and arranged for a more suitable suitor—Brandon—for his daughter. But Vicki and Ryan set their own plans in motion. Under the pretense of acting in accordance with Victor's wishes, Victoria set off for Chicago on a college-hunting venture with Brandon. The real reason for the trip: Victoria and Ryan's secret wedding.

Vicki sought solace in Ryan's arms.

Brandon swore himself to secrecy, but advised Vicki that the fake ID she produced was enough to render her marriage to Ryan illegal.

Victoria and Ryan wed in a secret
ceremony in Chicago.

Mr. and Mrs. Neil Winters

NEIL AND DRUCILLA:
A Chance Meeting

A fateful collision in the halls of Jabot brought up-and-coming junior executive Neil Winters and mailgirl Drucilla Barber together for the first time. She was in a pinch and had to produce a boyfriend for a double date, to cover up a little white lie she told to Nathan and Olivia. Neil obliged. Dru then realized that if she could hook up Neil and Olivia, her path to Nathan, to whom she was attracted, would be free and clear. Neil thought that he and Olivia would be a good match, but he also knew she was engaged to Nathan. When Drucilla danced for Neil, their on-again, off-again romance was suddenly on again. Their wedding took place in Katherine Chancellor's mansion, with Olivia and Brad serving as attendants to the bride and groom.

Top left: Neil fell for Olivia; Dru fell for Nathan. When Olivia and Nathan married, Dru and Neil made love on the rebound.

Center left: Neil gave Drucilla a "friendship" ring, but she knew it meant much more than that.

Bottom left: Neil's image of Drucilla changed when she danced, and he was hopelessly smitten.

Right: Dru and Neil honeymooned on the Caribbean island of Antigua.

Kristoff St. John's real-life father, Christopher St. John, acted as minister for Neil and Dru's wedding.

When Victoria Rowell (Dru) and Kristoff St. John (Neil) were scheduled to make a personal appearance in Antigua, Coordinating Producer Nancy Wiard worked some wizardry and managed to put together a last-minute location shoot.

RYAN AND NINA:
A Gigolo Grows Up

Nina, heiress to the Chancellor estate, used her money and her bed to catch the interest and eventually the heart of Ryan McNeil. Living the life of a "kept man" for a while, he proposed when he found out that Nina was expecting their baby. Though Ryan didn't feel the same intense love Nina did, he turned out to be good for her. He kept her focused on her college career while he tried to advance his own, and proved a suitable father for little Phillip Chancellor IV.

Nina discovered in Ryan a man who judged her on her own merits, not on her past mistakes.

At first, Little Phillip rejected Ryan. He later came to love him as his "daddy."

Despite their tumultuous beginnings, Ryan, Nina and little Phillip made a happy home life for themselves.

Neil and Christine stood up for Nina and Ryan when they wed.

Little Phillip gave his mother away in marriage to Ryan McNeil.

VICTORIA AND COLE:
My Brother, My Husband

Cole Howard, the handsome ranchhand Victor Newman hired, immediately caught the eye of Victor's daughter, Victoria. At first Cole rebuffed her advances because she was so young, but he finally realized that Victoria was the girl with whom he wanted to spend the rest of his life. He wrote his mother, Eve, the happy news, unaware that his mother had once had a relationship with Victor Newman. Eve was on a cruise when she received Cole's letter, and immediately determined that she must hurry to his side to keep him from marrying Victoria, whom she was sure was Cole's half sister. But Eve took ill and died before she could tell him her story. Meanwhile, Cole and Victoria secretly jetted off to Las Vegas for a quick wedding, and later consummated their vows. When they returned, Victor confronted them with the truth—they were brother and sister. The shocking news brought a reconciliation between Vicki and her mother, who also opposed the wedding. But how could she ever forgive her father for ruining her life? When the marriage was annulled, Vicki and Cole tried to get on with their lives. Victor, determined to get at the truth of Cole's parentage, ordered the exhumation of Eve's body and blood tests. To everyone's relief, he discovered that Cole and Victoria were not related after all and were free to remarry.

Young lovers Victoria and Cole met on the Newman Ranch, where Cole tended to the horses and wrote his first novel.

I know you had nothing but the highest respect for Victor ... and this news will be a blow. I'm sorry, Mother. We all miss him very much.

I do have some happier news. For the first time in my life, I've fallen in love. I've met the girl I want to marry, Mother --. She's a wonderful young woman, I know you'll love her, too. I have to say, I was caught very much off guard ... I never meant for this to happen, but it has happened-- She doesn't know herself yet, how deeply I feel about her. But mother, she's brought such joy to my life.

You'll be very surprised to hear who she is -- this young woman I'm so crazy about. Her name is Victoria. Victoria Newman. Victor's daughter.

Knowing how long you worked for him, and the respect you had for the man, I'm sure that will please you.

Cole's letter to his mother, in which he told her of his love for Victoria.

A defiant Victoria called her mother to inform her of her plans to marry Cole. Nikki was devastated that her daughter was marrying the man for whom she herself had fallen.

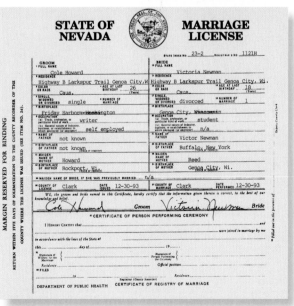

Eighteen-year-old Victoria believed that nothing could stand in the way of her and Cole living as husband and wife. They first married in Las Vegas.

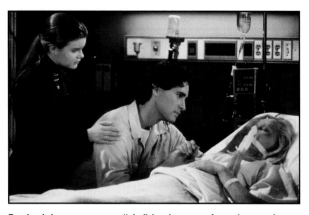

Eve's dying message, "sis," took on profound meaning when Victor revealed he was Cole's father.

IN THE
CIRCUIT COURT OF GENOA CITY
Chancery Division

IN RE: PETITION TO EXHUME)
     THE REMAINS OF)
     EVE HOWARD)
              Deceased,)   Case No. 94 CI-I
)
)

PETITION TO EXHUME REMAINS OF EVE HOWARD

Petitioner, VICTOR NEWMAN, respectfully represents unto this Honorable Court as follows:

1. Eve Howard, deceased, died, intestate, in the City of Genoa, County of Genoa, on or about the ___9___ day of __DEC.__, 1993.

2. She was thereafter buried in the __SERENITY MORTUARY__ in the County of Genoa.

3. By reason thereof the Court has jurisdiction of the subject matter of this Petition and, as more fully appears below, jurisdiction of the parties.

4. Eve Howard left one son, Cole Howard, surviving; Cole Howard is a resident of the City of Genoa City and the County of Genoa; Petitioner is aware of no other relatives and, to the best his information and belief , Eve Howard left no other relatives surviving.

5. Cole Howard is, by virtue of his relationship with Eve Howard, made a party hereto: as the attached papers demonstrate, he has been served with a copy of this Petition and with Notice of this Hearing.

6. Petitioner, who is a resident of the City of Genoa City and the County of Genoa, as well as others, have a vital interest in the resolution of certain personal matters which can only be resolved by genetic testing; should the Court deem it necessary and appropriate, Petitioner will provide the Court with a more definite statement of these interests.

7. Petitioner proposes, should the Court enter its Order authorizing the exhumation if the remains of Eve Howard, to have said remains transported to __GENOA CITY MEMORIAL__ where Dr. __MARK COHEN__ of __GENETICS DEPARTMENT__ will perform necessary testing.

8. Said testing will performed with a minimum disturbance of the remains of Eve Howard; specifically:

    A. at __G.C.M.H.__ where Dr. __MARK COHEN__ of __DEP. OF__ __GENETICS__ will remove a microscopic sample of __TISSUE__ from

Nina and Ryan served as matron of honor and best man at Cole and Victoria's second wedding.

Victoria couldn't forgive Victor for not leveling with her about Cole's questionable paternity, and refused to invite him to the second wedding. Victor, unseen by the bride and groom, stood disconsolately at the back of the church.

Despite a long and rocky road to the altar, Nicholas and Sharon finally became husband and wife.

NICHOLAS AND SHARON:
Putting Love to the Test

Nick and Sharon's friend Amy played a key role in freeing Nicholas from prison and ending their nightmare. She surprised them by agreeing to be a last-minute bridesmaid.

When Nicholas first met Sharon, she was all he could think about—morning, noon and night, day after day, week after week. The problem was that Sharon was Matt's girl, but she became as smitten with Nicholas as Nicholas was with her. Matt and Nicholas frequently came to blows over Sharon, and Nicholas found himself in deep trouble when he was arrested for shooting Matt—a crime he didn't commit—on the eve of his wedding to Sharon. While he was out on bond, the two young love-birds eloped, only to learn that the justice of the peace who married them was a fraud. Nicholas and Sharon were shattered when Nicholas was found guilty of attempted murder and sent to prison. Nicholas tried to get Sharon to go on with her life, but she stood by him—much to Nick's mother's chagrin. Nikki believed if it weren't for Sharon, Nicholas's life wouldn't be such a mess. When the charges were finally dropped and Nicholas was again a free man, he proposed to his beloved Sharon. This time, the wedding went off without a hitch, and they began their life together on the Newman Ranch.

Nikki had strong objections to Nick marrying Sharon, and threatened to disrupt the ceremony. If looks could kill...

Nicholas Newman and Sharon Collins Crowned King and Queen at Genoa City University Polynesian Dance

Sharon Collins and Nick Newman

"Justice of the Peace" Called Fraud

When Victor Newman paid for Sharon's mother's operation, Sharon was accused by Nikki and Victoria of wanting to sink her teeth into the Newman fortune.

Second-Time-Around Weddings

Rex and Katherine posed with young Phillip Chancellor and his fiancée, Cricket Blair, after their first wedding.

In real life as in the soaps, for better or worse, some people get a second chance on the marriage-go-round. It is simply amazing that after their first attempt, finding they could not live with each other, such couples had to go and do it again, because they could not live without each other! Three couples among all those restless second-timers best exemplify that need or desire for one more chance at making the magic work.

The bridal party added up to only one bride and one groom, a best man and a dejected matron of honor, plus family and close friends.

Jill negotiated with Katherine's minister to make it a double wedding ceremony.

Jill had some difficulty persuading Katherine to think that a bigger wedding was better.

Jill fantasized that John would be overwhelmed by her efforts to make it a day to remember.

KATHERINE CHANCELLOR AND REX STERLING:

"I'm Gonna Live Till I Die"

Katherine Chancellor and Rex Sterling first tripped to the altar in 1988, and no sooner had they recited their wedding vows than they were upstaged by wedding guest Nina Webster—she was soon to marry into the Chancellor family—who was going into labor. Forced to delay their honeymoon, Katherine and Rex spent their wedding night in the hospital waiting room for the arrival of what Nina termed their "wedding present." After a few years of wedded bliss for this unorthodox couple—who reveled in such fun things as hosting masquerade balls and other galas, taking a spin on a motorcycle whenever the spirit moved them, playing innocent games and tricks of one-upmanship on each other or dining by candlelight—they split over a huge misunderstanding. In the interim, Jill Foster Abbott, to whom Rex turned for consolation, managed to get him to a justice of the peace before Katherine had their marriage declared invalid.

Finally, in 1992, Rex resumed his courtship of Katherine, proposing to her in the Colonnade Room. Katherine accepted, Rex asked John to be his best man and Jill, who saw an opportunity to turn Katherine and Rex's wedding into something more, begged Katherine to designate her as matron of honor. Jill then went into action, managing to obtain a marriage license for herself and John and burying it in a pile of papers that John unwittingly signed at Jabot. Obtaining a copy of a recent blood test for John was also not too great a challenge. Just before the ceremony was to begin, Jill persuaded Katherine and Rex that a double wedding involving four old and good "friends" would be fantastic, and she assured them that the minister would be delighted to perform such a wedding. As for John Abbott, Jill argued, he would be so overwhelmed by the sheer romantic fantasy of it all that he would happily go along with the idea. Before the wedding ceremony began, Rex and Katherine set the mood by bursting into Katherine's favorite song, "I'm Gonna Live Till I Die." The only glitch was that John said he'd rather die than marry Jill, and the double ceremony didn't come off as Jill had planned.

John Abbott escorted his youngest child, Traci, down the aisle as she married Brad Carlton for the first time.

TRACI ABBOTT AND BRAD CARLTON:
Play It Again, Sam

In 1986, Traci Abbott married sexy Brad Carlton, the Abbott family's groundskeeper. Traci, the epitome of the poor little rich girl, had already had a spate of emotional as well as physical problems, and had to learn to love herself before she could experience mature love. Traci and Brad's marital problems seemed to begin when Brad disappeared, leading Traci to believe her husband had deserted her. When he returned, Traci was in the process of filing for a divorce. Other problems also kept these two young people apart, not the least of which were Brad's consuming ambition to swiftly climb the corporate ladder—he had much greater goals than remaining the family's groundskeeper—and his eye for beautiful women, notably Lauren Fenmore and Traci's sister, Ashley. As if Brad's plate were not totally full, Traci, after a year's absence from Genoa City, decided to move back home, determined to win him back. In 1991, Brad and Traci remarried after she became pregnant. Although the birth of their daughter, Colleen, was not the bonding agent Traci had hoped it would be for their shaky marriage, Traci would forever be connected to Brad through their daughter.

After their marriage, the two young lovers had eyes only for each other.

Clockwise from top:

After Traci and Brad wed for the second time, Ashley and Victor toasted the bride and groom.

Traci accepted her father's best wishes for the second wedding as Brad looked on.

Jill caught the bridal bouquet. Should John watch out?

Traci posed with her parents, John and Dina; her brother and sister, Jack and Ashley; Mamie; and Jill.

JILL FOSTER AND JOHN ABBOTT:
If at First We Mess It Up...

In 1982, John Abbott married Jill Foster. Jack was his father's best man and Jill's mother, Liz Foster, was matron of honor.

John Abbott took an immediate liking to Jill Foster, the girl his son Jack was dating. And the more he saw of her, and she him, the more they were attracted to each other. Jill was quite a number of years younger than John, but the excitement and fulfillment she brought to his life made him feel like a kid again. It wasn't long before John proposed to Jill, and they married in the fall of 1982. The couple found much happiness in their marriage, although John's grown children and his longtime faithful maid, Mamie, were not too fond of Jill and seemed to bring out her worst traits. One night John and Jill quarreled, and Jill, in a fit of temper, fled the house and found comfort in the arms of another man—John's own son, Jack. When John found out about her indiscretion, he sued for divorce, and then left for New York City where he spent more than a year trying to mend his broken heart. Upon his return, Jill once again tried to rekindle the old flame, but John would not be fooled again. Gradually, however, Jill worked her way into John's heart and home. She convinced him that not only did she truly love him, but that he couldn't bear to live without her. With Rex Sterling as best man and Katherine Chancellor as matron of honor, the two lovers tied the knot for a second time in an impromptu ceremony in the Abbotts' living room. They were confident that this time they would get it right.

Multiple choice question:
Select the most appropriate answer.

By marrying Jill Foster for the second time on January 7, 1992, John Abbott was making the following statement:
- **A.** I know I'm alive when I'm with Jill because my heart starts to pound and my pulse races.
- **B.** I remember how close Jill and my son Jack once were.
- **C.** I'm going to have to tell Mamie I'll no longer need to drink ginseng tea.
- **D.** I'm looking forward to spending a lot of quiet evenings at home with Jill, putting jigsaw puzzles together.
- **E.** I truly believe, "Love is better, the second time around."

Rex, Katherine and Mamie flank the bride and groom.

In 1992, both Jill and John had their feet on the ground for marriage Number 2 and the happy couple looked forward to happily ever-aftering.

MOST MEMORABLE

Couples

Throughout the years, "The Young and the Restless" has

introduced viewers to many memorable couples. For some

couples, there is one specific moment that defines their

relationship. For others, there are a series of memorable

moments that seem to follow one after another, spanning

the length of their relationship. And yet for others, it is

simply the fact that they are inextricably tied together, for

life and beyond, that makes them truly memorable.

Jed oversaw Lorie's career as a novelist and accompanied her on her booksigning tour.

LORIE BROOKS & JED ANDREWS

Jed Andrews was Lorie Brooks's old flame. A certain magnetism drew them together, and threatened to break up Jed's already failing marriage. But Jed was more, much more than Lorie's lover. He was also a critical player in her quest to achieve success as a novelist. For it was Jed who managed to get her first manuscript to a New York publisher, helped her secure a lucrative contract for the book and got producers in Hollywood interested in its potential for the big screen. When Lorie's engagement to Brad ended over her involvement in Leslie's breakdown, it was Jed who comforted her. He toured with her to promote the book and later negotiated another publishing deal for Lorie, this time for her autobiographical exposé, *In My Sister's Shadow*.

One of the most memorable moments in Lorie and Jed's relationship came when the two lovers shared a steamy, soapy shower. Actors Jaime Lyn Bauer and Tom Selleck made soap opera history in what was referred to at the time as the most erotic, steamiest, sexiest scene ever to be seen on the daytime suds!

LANCE PRENTISS & LORIE BROOKS

Leslie Brooks arranged a date for her sister, self-confident and independent Lorie, with equally self-confident and equally independent millionaire Lance Prentiss. It was like spontaneous combustion when the two finally connected. The prospect of the chase thrilled them, and each was certain they could make the other be the first to relent. When their game-playing became so intense that they fell in love, Lance romanced Lorie to the extreme—jetting to exotic adventures all over the world and spending evenings sipping expensive champagne. Yet there was one important caveat to their relationship: no sex until after they were married. This, too, became part of the attraction, with Lorie doing everything she could to make Lance crave her as much as she wanted him. What Lorie didn't bargain for was the stiff competition for Lance's affections from his mother, Vanessa, whose passion for her son bordered on the incestuous, and from the very woman who had set them up, her sister Leslie.

Millionaire Lance Prentiss and novelist Lorie Brooks shared a volatile, passionate love in the early years of "The Young and the Restless."

BRAD ELIOT & LESLIE BROOKS

Introvert Leslie Brooks was consumed by her budding career as a concert pianist. When she met Brad Eliot, a reporter who worked for her father's newspaper, she found a true friend. They spent countless hours together, conversing and getting to know one another. Lorie, always the jealous sister, decided she would make Brad hers, for no other reason than that Leslie had fallen deeply in love with him. Through Lorie's interference, Leslie began to think Brad was losing interest in her, and Brad felt Leslie was placing her career above their relationship. Devastated over the news that Lorie and Brad were spending the evening together in bed, Leslie suffered a breakdown in the middle of a concert performance. When Brad discovered it was Lorie's involvement that triggered Leslie's collapse, he rushed to her side. Leslie recovered and her dream came true. She and Brad were married.

Shy, fragile Leslie Brooks allowed herself to open up and to fall in love with her handsome friend, Brad Eliot.

Brad helped Leslie recover from her breakdown, and the two were wed.

The lovers didn't utter a word. The music said it all.

In one of the most memorable moments in the history of "The Young and the Restless," Lance Prentiss and Leslie Brooks "silently" shared their feelings through lyric, story and emotion. As viewers witnessed them sharing a cup of tea and meaningful glances, they also heard the two "singing" to one another "Until It's Time for You to Go." Echoing the lyrics, Lance approached the door to leave, but one more look at Leslie was enough to remind him that their love "has no beginning, it has no end." As the music reached a crescendo, their emotions spilled over and the scene ended in a passionate embrace, a final consummation of their relationship after many years of longing.

LESLIE BROOKS & LANCE PRENTISS

Struggling Liz Foster and wealthy publisher Stuart Brooks survived his indiscretion with her daughter, Jill, and became husband and wife.

LIZ FOSTER & STUART BROOKS

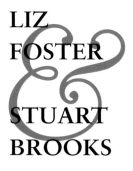

It was the classic love story of the poor working girl falling in love with and marrying the rich boy from the right side of the tracks. But it was played out here in the mature love story of Liz Foster and Stuart Brooks. Liz Foster, a blue-collar working mother, struggled to provide for her children: manicurist Jill, medical student Snapper and fledgling lawyer Greg. Her relationship with Stuart ran into troubled waters when Jill attempted to steal Stuart away from her mother. Once Stuart set things right again, he proposed to Liz and she accepted. On their wedding day, Liz and Stuart became grandparents when Chris Foster gave birth to her first child, Jennifer (after Stuart's deceased wife) Elizabeth Foster. The Foster and Brooks clans were bound together through the strength of this union.

Paul met Cindy at the Golden Touch when he went undercover to find out who framed his father, Detective Carl Williams, who had been trying to break up the vice racket in Genoa City. A true hooker with a heart of gold, Cindy decided to help Paul crack the syndicate and the two fell in love. For that love, Cindy would do any-thing, including putting her own life in jeopardy to protect Paul. When Paul proposed marriage, Cindy could scarcely believe that all her dreams were coming true. But as fate would have it, their life together was not to be. Everything ended when Cindy stepped in front of Paul, taking a bullet intended for him.

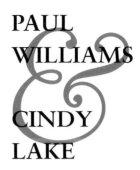

PAUL WILLIAMS & CINDY LAKE

Saying good-bye to Paul, the dying Cindy told him that her happiest moments were those she had spent with him.

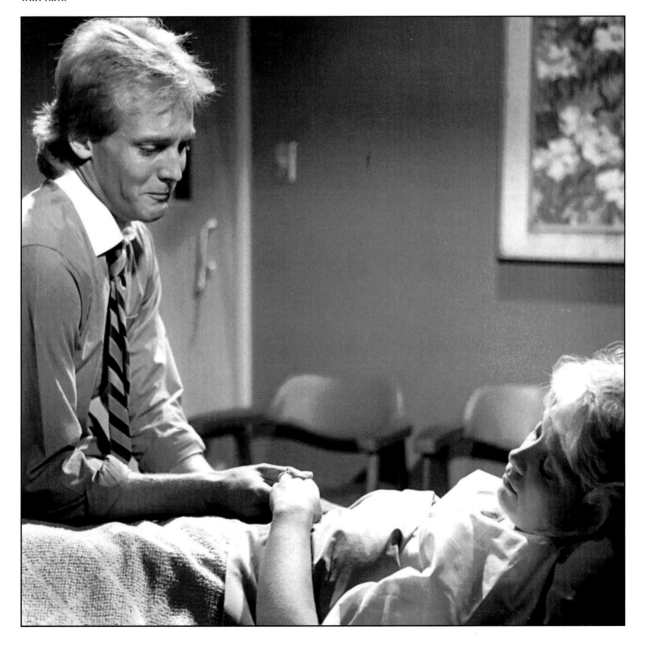

ASHLEY ABBOTT & STEVEN LASSITER

It was Dr. Steven Lassiter who nursed Ashley Abbott back to complete physical and emotional health, enabling her to start rebuilding her life. As her treatment progressed, Dr. Lassiter began taking a more than professional interest in his patient. When he proposed marriage, Ashley accepted. She knew she could count on Steven to always be there for her when she needed him. But the comfortable and secure life they were building came to an abrupt and tragic end when Steven was fatally shot by the son of a patient, who blamed him for his mother's death.

Ashley married Steven and loved him, but their marriage was short-lived.

John gave his daughter away in a small ceremony at the Abbott family home.

Lauren Fenmore and Paul Williams made better friends than lovers. They married when they were young, but Lauren's desire for a singing career and Paul's dream of a family put them at odds. Their union was marked by many memorable moments. One of the most shocking was when Paul saw his wife "making love" to her ex-fiancé, Danny Romalotti, in a music video. Paul didn't appreciate her explanation that she was "acting." But they shared an extraordinarily tender moment when Paul gave Lauren the engagement ring he could not afford to give her earlier.

Paul and Lauren finally divorced when she ran off with her psychotic manager, Shawn. Once Lauren returned, the couple almost reconciled but they realized once and for all that they had very different goals and they shared a tearful good-bye.

LAUREN FENMORE & PAUL WILLIAMS

Lauren and Paul would always be there for each other—as friends, not as lovers.

JACK & NIKKI ABBOTT

Jack Abbott was Nikki's rock during her bouts with back trouble and alcoholism, and he was always there for Nikki and her children. He even loved Nicholas as if he were his own son. But Nikki was Jack's passion, and he would do anything to keep her in his life. So distraught was he over the prospect that she was going to break it off with him and return to Victor, that Jack crashed his car and was rushed to the hospital. On her way to visit him, Nikki's doctor congratulated her on her pregnancy! Having already miscarried once, Nikki knew she now had another chance to give Jack his own child—the one dream that meant more to him than anything. How could she take that away from this man for whom she cared so deeply? Nikki sacrificed a future with Victor to start a family with Jack. In a confrontation with Victor over their daughter, Victoria, Nikki accidentally fell down the stairs, jeopardizing the baby's life. Tragically, Nikki and Jack's baby was born prematurely and died, and they both agreed to donate the baby's organs so that another child might live. All of Jack's emotions came rushing back to him as, in one of the most heartrending moments ever on "The Young and the Restless," he held the baby whose life was saved by the donation of his son's heart.

Nikki brought out Jack's sensitive side; Jack provided stability for Nikki and her children, but she still carried a torch for Victor.

ASHLEY ABBOTT & VICTOR NEWMAN

Victor loved to shower Ashley with gifts.

Victor's penchant for rescuing beautiful damsels in distress brought him and Ashley Abbott together. When Ashley learned that Brent Davis was her real father, it so traumatized her that she wandered out into the rain-swept highway, nearly getting hit by a truck. Disoriented to the point of not knowing who she was, Ashley ended up at a truck stop diner and became a waitress. Victor saved her from being violated by a surly truck driver, and took Ashley home with him, vowing to nurse her back to health. Victor and Ashley's romance continued for years, with Victor always there for her through one trauma after another. One day the two lovers came upon an old, abandoned cabin in the woods, which Ashley romantically adopted as their "special" place. In the blink of an eye, Victor had the cabin completely refurbished for Ashley. Eventually Victor and Nikki divorced. Victor's chance finally came and he married his beautiful Ashley, a woman for whom he would continue to have a special love and friendship, even after their marriage had ended.

LAUREN FENMORE & BRAD CARLTON

Even though Lauren Fenmore was attracted to Brad Carlton, she knew Brad loved Traci and wanted to win her back from Tim Sullivan. So when Brad regained his strength after his ordeal with his ex-wife Lisa, Lauren and Scott cooked up a scheme. They made Brad look desperately ill, and Lauren phoned Traci, frantic, saying she'd better get to the hospital fast...or it might be too late. Traci fell for the story, and eventually she and Brad did get back together.

It wasn't a hoax the next time Traci found Lauren at Brad's bedside. With Traci in New York with Steve Connelly and Colleen, Lauren and Brad's steamy affair heated up. The wild Ms. Fenmore was too much for Brad to handle, though, and he suffered a heart attack in her bed.

Fenmore Snatches Newman Top Exec.

LAUREN FENMORE and BRADLEY CARLTON

Brad could often be found in Lauren's bed—or in a hospital bed with her by his side.

Brad saw more than one opportunity at Fenmore's, so he resigned his post at Newman Enterprises and went to work for Lauren.

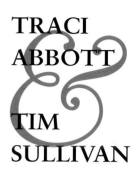
Traci Abbott got more of an education than she bargained for when her college professor, Tim Sullivan, took his lessons out of the classroom and into the bedroom. When the innocent young Traci lost her virginity to Tim, she got pregnant. Running to Tim's apartment to tell him the happy news, she was devastated to discover him carrying on with another woman. The distraught Traci turned to her good friend Danny Romalotti, who married her to give her baby a name.

Traci Abbott was not the first coed with whom Professor Tim Sullivan was involved, nor was she the last.

Much to Brad's dismay, Traci and Tim's relationship rekindled several years later, when he encouraged her to go to graduate school and pursue writing. Traci's brother, Jack, tolerated Tim because he detested Brad.

CAROL ROBBINS & SKIP EVANS

Carol and Skip decided to take it slow. They were a good match, but Carol wasn't sure Skip would be comfortable living his life with a handicapped woman—Carol wore a leg brace as a result of a childhood illness. As they continued to grow closer, Skip was able to prove that he loved Carol for who she was, and assured her that her disability never got in their way. With the support and love of the Abbott family, Skip and Carol had a fairy-tale wedding. Soon after the marriage, Carol's doctors told them that having a baby would not put her health in jeopardy. But starting a family proved difficult for the couple. Skip, they found out, couldn't father a child, and adoption agencies rejected them because of Carol's disability. Desperate to become parents, they took out an ad in the newspaper, and Nan, a young, pregnant college student, responded and moved into their home. After the baby was born, however, Nan had a change of heart about giving up her baby. She reestablished a relationship with the baby's father, and won a court battle to get her baby back. But the young couple soon realized that raising their daughter was too much for them to handle, so they returned baby Skylar to Carol and Skip, certain she would grow up in a loving home.

Carol's disability never got in the way of Skip's loving her.

Unbeknownst to the Evanses, baby Skylar's biological mother watched the christening and set her sights on getting her daughter back.

OLIVIA & NATHAN HASTINGS

The happy news that Olivia was expecting the baby she and Nathan so desperately wanted was tempered by the diagnosis that Olivia was suffering from a severe condition that was a precursor to uterine cancer. Afraid of Nathan's reaction, she kept the news to herself, fearing this might be her only chance to conceive, and even though she knew she was putting her own life at risk, she resolved to carry the baby to term. After celebrating Olivia's pregnancy, Nathan came across her medical records. Grief stricken, he maintained a brave front and kept silent. When Olivia overheard Nathan discussing her condition with Mamie, she confronted him, and he assured her that together they would make it through the difficult months ahead. As Olivia's condition worsened, she was hospitalized, and the doctor induced labor in a valiant effort to save both mother and child. Thankfully, Olivia and baby Nate came through the ordeal, and she felt her shaky marriage was finally on more solid ground. Until, that is, Nathan's indiscretions would once again put the lives of his family in jeopardy.

Dr. Olivia Hastings struggled to regain control of her life during and after her medical trauma.

Family friend Katherine Chancellor met baby Nate, whose entrance into the world almost cost Olivia her life.

CRICKET BLAIR & SCOTT GRAINGER

Cricket Blair was more than a little surprised when, while looking through her boyfriend Scott's photo album, she found a picture of a man—Scott's father—who strongly resembled a picture she had of her father. When Dr. James Grainger visited Genoa City, Scott insisted on introducing the girl he was falling in love with to his dad. Convinced Jim was her father, Cricket confronted him, but he said he knew nothing about a young girl in Kansas (Cricket's mother, Jessica), who met a boy and got pregnant, only to never see him again. At Cricket's 20th birthday party, Jessica and Jim found themselves face to face. Jim finally admitted that he was, in fact, Jessica's young lover. Neither of them ever knew that his letters had been intercepted by Jessica's mother. In a cruel twist of fate, Cricket, who had just been presented with an engagement ring, learned that her fiancé was also her half brother!

Cricket and Scott's romance was cut short just in time when they found out they were brother and sister.

CASSANDRA RAWLINS & BRAD CARLTON

Cassandra and Brad made a beautiful couple.

Brad Carlton had no recollection of marrying Cassandra Rawlins. The widow Rawlins had been wooing Brad to not only head up her Ra-Tech corporation, but to be CEO in the love department as well. When Brad rebuffed her attempts at both, she drugged him and they jetted off to Las Vegas, where their flight attendant served as witness to their wedding. Shocked and angry at first, Brad decided to give the marriage a chance when word of the union leaked to the press. It took only a couple of months for them to divorce. Or so they thought. It seems the judge died before he had a chance to actually sign the papers, so even though Paul Williams was named the sole heir to Cassie's fortune when she met an untimely death, Brad Carlton became a very wealthy man when the fortune reverted to him.

Brad didn't remember marrying Cassandra, or signing the marriage certificate.

VICTOR & NEWMAN HOPE ADAMS

Feeling rejected by his family, Victor Newman took off for parts unknown on a mission to find himself. His life changed when he rescued a blind woman about to be attacked by one of her farmhands. That woman, Hope Adams, softened Victor's harshness as he helped her recover from her injuries and tended to her farm. But Hope was disillusioned when she accompanied Victor to Genoa City and saw how ruthless he was in business. She returned to Kansas and Victor followed, declaring his love for her. When Hope questioned his ability to deal with her blindness, he shocked her by proposing. After their marriage, Hope got pregnant and they both worried that their child might also be blind. But Hope insisted on having the baby, and Victor Adam Newman Jr. was born sighted. Although each loved and respected the other, it had become apparent to both Victor and Hope that their marriage couldn't survive their many differences. Hope didn't fit into his world, and Victor could never be the husband that she needed. Hope decided to return to her farm and raise their child there.

Hope had no idea of Victor's wealth and power when she met him on her farm in Kansas.

Victor's life in Genoa City couldn't have been more different than Hope's, but they shared many things, including humble beginnings in orphanages.

Douglas Austin befriended Hope and approved of her relationship with his best friend, Victor.

Victor taught Hope how to dance. She taught him much more.

Victor found a special love in an
extraordinary woman named Hope.

Nikki crashed Hope and Victor's
wedding reception.

HOPE NEWMAN & CLIFF WILSON

Hope and Cliff were both kind, honest, sensitive people living simple lives. They had always loved each other and planned to marry, but Hope called off the wedding because of her feelings for Victor. Cliff felt he could never compete with a man like Victor Newman, so he tried to get on with his life. But when Hope rushed to Cliff's side after he was seriously injured in a farming accident, Cliff realized how deep his feelings for Hope still were. After Hope had Victor's baby and realized she couldn't live in his world, she headed back to Kansas and married Cliff, who would be a loving father to Victor's son.

Cliff always loved Hope, and that love won out when Victor and Hope's marriage dissolved.

Hope helped nurse Cliff back to health, and then mended his broken heart.

Mari Jo was a good friend to Jack—someone he could turn to in happiness and sorrow. She hoped his feelings would run deeper than friendship.

MARI JO MASON & JACK ABBOTT

Was she Mari Jo Mason, or someone named Marilyn with a hidden past? Regardless, Jack Abbott found her to be a good listener—someone he could finally open up to about his experience in Vietnam— and she responded with great sensitivity. Mari Jo fell deeply in love with Jack and he proposed, just at the time Jack rediscovered his long-lost love, Luan, whom he planned to whisk away on a romantic Caribbean vacation. Mari Jo bared her claws by telling Luan, her number-one obstacle to happiness with Jack, that Jack was only being kind to her out of obligation. Hurt but grateful for Mari Jo's womanly insight, naive Luan backed out of the trip and Jack went alone. Mari Jo soon followed and they frolicked in the sun and surf, but Jack, torn between her and Luan, broke off their engagement. After Luan and Jack married, Luan confided in Mari Jo about her illness, and asked her to look after Jack when she was gone. In his grief Jack turned to Mari Jo, because he knew her love for him was still strong. In the end, however, Mari Jo's love became so obsessive that it not only killed their romance—it destroyed her as well.

Mari Jo followed Jack to St. Thomas, but couldn't get him to marry her. His heart belonged to his first love, Luan.

Star-crossed lovers Chris and Paul had their share of troubles on the way to the altar.

CHRISTINE BLAIR & PAUL WILLIAMS

Good guy detective Paul Williams was there to help Christine pick up the pieces after Danny broke her heart. They grew closer and fell in love, but a hit-and-run accident on their way to the altar left Paul impotent. Paul felt he was doing the noble thing by calling off the wedding, but Chris's heart was broken once again. Their working relationship continued: his crime solving and her "legal eagleing" went hand in hand, and soon they were heart to heart again. The stage was set for wedding Number 2, but this time it was Chris's betrayal of Paul that dashed their dreams. When Chris convinced Paul she had finally closed the Danny chapter of her life, they set about making wedding plans again, and bought a condo together. This time the star-crossed lovers did marry.

CHRISTINE BLAIR

Hit and run accident is still at large. Police are hoping than an eye witness will provide them with some clues as to the kind of car was used.

Many persons feel at this stage that some legal action is forthcoming but it now be-

PAUL WILLIAMS

Of no less importance was the common recognition shown of the fact that any menace from without to the peace of our continents concerns all of us and therefore properly is a subject for consultation and cooperation. This was reflected in the in-

Miss Christine Blair

and

Mr. Paul Williams

request that you join them

as they celebrate their marriage

and for the reception

immediately afterward at

Christ Church

Chris and Paul's wedding guests were gathered when they received word the bride and groom were injured in a hit-and-run accident.

Chris and Paul's wedding plans were all in place... again. But it was not to be.

Miss Christine Blair

and

Mr. Paul Williams

request the honour of your presence

at their marriage

on

Wednesday, the fourteenth of February

nineteen hundred and ninety-six

at half after five o'clock

Chapel of the Good Shepherd

Genoa City, Wisconsin

MOST MEMORABLE
Triangles

We all know there are many kinds of tri-angles. There's the geometric kind we learned about in school. There's the three-sided drawing or drafting guide used by draftsmen and architects. There's the musi-cal percussion instrument. And then there's the most common kind of all: the relation-ship triangle involving three (or sometimes even four) people. You know, a child caught in the middle between two bicker-ing parents. Or a parent opposing two young lovers. Or two allies at odds with a third party. The combinations are endless. We encounter people-relationship triangles all the time in real life. They are also the lifeline of the soaps. But the most com-pelling of all soap triangles are the love tri-angles, which keep us mesmerized and glued to the screen as we make connections between fact and fantasy.

CHRIS ▲ SNAPPER ▲ SALLY

Chris Brooks's moral stance to not engage in physical love with Snapper before marriage made him turn to Sally McGuire, a beautiful young waitress whom he met at the Allegro. Sally's deep love for Snapper resulted in something which she decided to keep secret. When Snapper told Sally he had decided to marry Chris, she was heartbroken. But to give her unborn child a name, she later accepted the marriage proposal of Pierre Roulland, owner of the Allegro. Sally's secret, however, was discovered by Pierre's smothering sister, Marianne, and it gave her a weapon to use against Sally, should the right moment occur. That "moment" arrived shortly afterward when there was a robbery in the restaurant and Pierre was killed. When Sally's baby was born, Marianne flew straight to the Brooks family, disclosing that Snapper was the father. While this revelation seriously tested Snapper's marriage to Chris, their great love for each other got them over this hurdle, and they began to erect a united front against any and all of the challenges the future might hold.

Chris and Snapper were very much in love, but he wasn't ready for marriage, and she wasn't ready for intimacy.

Snapper frequently saw Sally McGuire at the Allegro where she waitressed. They became very close friends.

Right: Sally contemplated her pregnancy, a secret she kept from Snapper so as not to destroy his marriage to Chris.

After Pierre's unfortunate death, Snapper regularly visited Sally at the hospital, as she awaited the birth of their child.

Pierre Roulland, Sally's boss, offered her a way out of her dilemma: marriage to give her unborn child a name.

KATHERINE ▲ PHILLIP ▲ JILL

The man, the nemesis, and the wife.

Never in Jill's wildest dreams would she have imagined she could be so lucky! Wealthy socialite Katherine Chancellor had just offered her the opportunity to live in her mansion as her personal girl Friday. Her eyes sparkling with girlish excitement, coupled with the unbounded devotion she felt toward her benefactress, the 18-year-old surveyed her new surroundings, a beautiful mansion filled with expensive furniture and lavish accouterments, set in the lush surroundings of a country farmland estate. It took her breath away! Jill vowed always to be true to Mrs. Chancellor—she wanted so much to help her conquer her terrible drinking problem. Katherine's husband, Phillip, a fine soft-spoken gentleman, had long ago retreated from the closeness he once shared with his wife. And although he still loved her, Phillip couldn't stand their senseless arguments over her heavy drinking and smoking. He noticed how patient Jill was and on many an occasion, his heart went out to the poor girl for the abuse Katherine heaped upon her. As time passed, Jill and Phillip became close friends; it was more an unspoken alliance of two souls uniting to meet a common challenge. One night, Phillip appeared in the doorway of Jill's room. It was a powerful moment when their common bond stripped away all their defenses and they made love.

In the presence of her family, Jill married the dying Phillip to give the baby she was carrying the Chancellor name.

A few months later, Phillip found out Jill was pregnant. He demanded a "quickie" divorce from Katherine, which he would obtain in the Dominican Republic. In a gesture of friendship, Katherine picked him up at the airport upon his return. They were making small talk when suddenly Katherine, rounding a dangerous mountain curve, pressed her foot down hard on the accelerator and sent the car sailing over a cliff. Katherine survived, but Phillip was not as lucky. As he lay dying in his hospital bed, he had one last request to make of his beloved Jill: marry him to give their unborn child his name and his fortune!

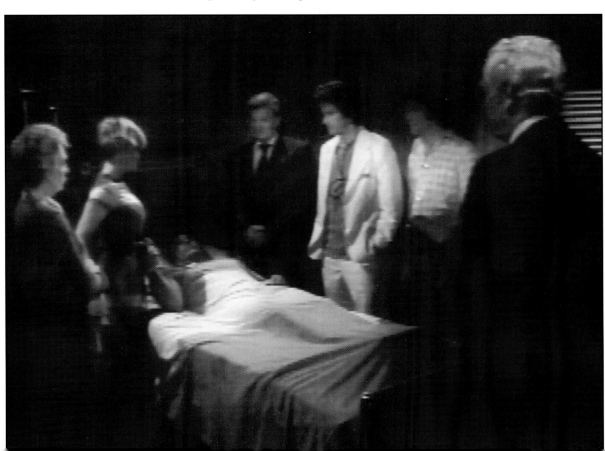

Handsome Eric Garrison was caught in a vise between two women, alluring businesswoman Ashley Abbott, and the successful, sophisticated femme fatale, Madame Mergeron.

DINA ▲ ERIC ▲ ASHLEY

Parisian Eric Garrison first met Ashley Abbott when Madame Mergeron asked him to travel to Genoa City to investigate the feasibility of buying out Jabot. Ashley's brother, Jack, led Garrison on, and made him believe that such a buyout was a real possibility, causing John Abbott to have a heart attack when he was told about it. Likewise having an attack of the heart, Ashley fell head over heels for the handsome Frenchman, who asked her to marry him before he was called back for an early return to Paris. John Abbott, meanwhile, had changed his mind about selling out, and indicated he was now ready to explore the matter more seriously. As the talks progressed to the point of closing the deal, Madame Mergeron—to Eric's great surprise—insisted upon being present for the closing. All of the Abbotts awaited her arrival, and, in a stunning moment, she revealed herself! Under the heavily veiled hat was the long-absent Dina Abbott, John's first wife and the mother of his children. To further complicate matters, daughter Ashley, who of all the children most resented their mother, learned that Dina had had an affair with Eric and was unwilling to surrender her former lover. Ashley fled to Paris to make up her mind about whether she would accept Eric's proposal. Upon her return, she told Eric she would marry him, and in the process, broke her mother's heart. But on the day of the wedding, Ashley called it off.

(Clockwise) Two brothers, Lucas and Lance, and two sisters, Lorie and Leslie—the "Four L's".

LANCE ▲ LORIE ▲ LESLIE ▲ LUCAS

They were labeled the "Four L's": Lance and Lucas (Prentiss) and Leslie and Lorie (Brooks). Two brothers in love with two sisters. Problems loomed for the foursome when one of the brothers or one of the sisters longed for the other sibling's lover, lousing up what otherwise could have been a lasting friendship. Lance, with his lady-killer good looks, married luscious, if loquacious, Lorie, after levelheaded, low-key Leslie threw them together when Lorie was longing for someone who lamentably was off-limits to her. After Lance and Lucas's mother Vanessa's longtime labors to split up Lance and Lorie resulted in Lance's leaving Lorie, the lovelorn Leslie let down her defenses and landed in Lance's bed. Their night of love would produce a son, Brooks, a secret that Leslie, ever the lady, would keep from Lance upon learning of Lance's intentions to go back to Lorie. It was then that loner Lucas leaped forward, offering to marry Leslie to legitimize her baby, even though Lucas secretly lusted after Lorie, whom he would later marry. And so the four L's would continue their living, loving and lusting with a largesse of style, grace and class.

Lance and Lorie fell madly in love after a whirlwind, but stormy, courtship.

Lucas lusted after Lorie.

Vanessa preferred to have the docile Leslie rather than Lorie in her sons' lives.

JILL ▴ DEREK ▴ KATHERINE

After the death of the love of her life, Phillip Chancellor, Jill thought she'd never fall in love again. Then one fateful day she wandered into a rather ordinary-looking beauty shop and laid eyes upon Derek Thurston, the Adonis who owned it. It was love at first sight for Jill. She asked Derek if he needed a beautician to help him in his expanding business, and they soon were working side by side. As their friendship deepened, he shared his most cherished dream with her to one day operate a salon that would cater to the crème de la crème. Crafty Jill came up with a plan for Derek to realize his dream, and for her to extract revenge against Katherine Chancellor! She advised him to cultivate the friendship of her old, dear, very wealthy and very lonely "friend." The one thing Jill didn't count on was that Derek would arouse the same longings in Katherine as he had stirred up in her. In no time at all Katherine was Derek's partner in the Golden Comb and in his bed.

What Derek couldn't remember was how Katherine had manipulated him into marrying her when he was in a drunken stupor. Crushed that he had no memory at all of their marriage, Katherine lied at first, saying they had only slept together—no strings attached. But when Jill decided to fight for the man she loved, Katherine produced the marriage certificate and promised that hell would freeze over before she'd let Jill have Derek! Katherine cut an ironclad deal with her husband: in exchange for one year of his life, he would live platonically with her; she would set up a $100,000 trust fund for Jill's son, Phillip; and then Katherine would give Derek his freedom plus sole ownership in the Golden Comb. Certain that Katherine would contest the divorce he so desperately wanted and make sure it would be messy and long—with no payback—Derek agreed. Once again, Katherine won and Jill walked away, telling Derek it was just too painful for her to stick around.

Katherine had so ingratiated herself with Derek that he was soon captivated by her wealth and charm.

Derek Thurston thought he could have it all—Jill, the woman he loved and Katherine, his benefactress.

Gina and Neil's chance at happiness ended on the very day that they were to be wed.

GINA ▲ NEIL ▲ JOANNA

Gina Roma, proprietor of Gina's Place, could hardly believe what was happening: she not only was in love with Neil Fenmore, debonair CEO of Fenmore Department Stores, but he was also in love with her! As their wedding day was fast approaching, she could hardly believe she was going to become Neil Fenmore's bride—it was a dream come true. She was sublimely unaware of the behind-the-scenes forces conspiring against their marriage: JoAnna, Neil's former wife, who had vague hopes of reconciling with her ex; a woman named Frances; and Neil's daughter Lauren Fenmore Williams, who schemed with her mother to tear the two lovers apart on the very day of their wedding! Anxious to make her wedding day the first day of the rest of her life, Gina had kept certain facts from her past secret. Frances disclosed to Neil that she had been Gina's cell mate for three years in a New York State prison! That was enough for Neil. He could not forgive or forget that Gina hadn't been honest with him. It wasn't only the deed, but how he found out about it, so he called the wedding off. Several days later, a heavy-hearted Neil wandered into Gina's Place and took a table in a darkened nook. Hurting as much as he, Gina was singing the mournful words of the torch song, "The Man That Got Away." As the last notes faded, Neil stood up, hesitated a moment, and then headed for the door without looking back.

TRACI ▲ DANNY ▲ LAUREN

Struggling rock singer Danny Romalotti found himself wedged between two young women, each of whom would stop at little to win his affections. First, there was shy, private Traci Abbott, who was painfully sensitive over her generous size and her perceived lack of beauty. When Danny came into the picture, Traci was immediately smitten, and she uncharacteristically went into action to stake her claim. For starters, she canceled her plans to go away to college, went on a crash diet, became president of Danny's fan club, attended his concerts and reveled in the applause she received when she sang with him. In short, she was putting up a good fight for her man. But then there was Traci's "good friend," Lauren Fenmore, whose own share of hangups manifested themselves in a much different way. Publicly nice and secretly obnoxious to Traci, the beguiling Lauren set out to steal Danny from right under Traci's nose and became engaged to him. She would later drop Danny like a hot potato when she fell in love with Paul Williams. By this time, Traci, too, had turned her attention elsewhere, concentrating on her studies.

While caught between Traci and Lauren, Danny would rather have chosen his longtime love, Patty Williams, who had married womanizer Jack Abbott.

JAZZ ▲ AMY ▲ TYRONE

There were no two brothers more unalike than Jazz and Tyrone Jackson. Jazz was a big hulk of a man, an ex-con who could not seem to go straight even though he had a strong motivation to do so. He lived in a sparse, shabby apartment because he was using all of his money to keep his handsome, younger brother, Tyrone, enrolled in law school in New York City. Then Tyrone got word that he would be spending his summer vacation working in the County Prosecutor's office in Genoa City, in a job Jazz had wanted. Moreover, Tyrone informed his brother he'd be moving in with him.

It wasn't long before Jazz introduced Tyrone to "his woman," Amy Lewis, the daughter of Frank Lewis, who headed Genoa City's law enforcement department. But Amy didn't know how to tell Jazz that she was not as much in love with him as he was with her. Besides, her father didn't want his daughter dating an ex-con, and he felt Tyrone would be a more suitable match.

Soon the brothers were working at cross-purposes. Jazz was ordered by the mob to eliminate his own brother, Tyrone, who, disguised as Leon Monroe, was working out of the County Prosecutor's office to break the syndicate headed by Mr. Anthony. Amy perceived that Tyrone was getting in deeper with the mob, so she put herself in the precarious position of posing as a hooker, nearly blowing Tyrone's cover. Amy confessed her love for Tyrone to Jazz, who realized how easy it would be to carry

Amy was Jazz's woman, but Tyrone loved her, too, and of the two brothers, Amy loved Tyrone best.

out the mob's instructions to execute Tyrone and win back Amy. But Jazz truly loved his brother, and he was able to substitute the body of a dead drug pusher of approximately the same size and build as Tyrone, who had been shot in the face, for the Leon Monroe he had to eliminate. To top it off, he slipped a pendant Amy had given Tyrone into the bag containing the personal effects of the dead man. When Amy insisted upon accompanying her father to the morgue to identify the supposedly dead Tyrone, she collapsed in grief in her father's arms when she saw the pendant. Mr. Anthony, who witnessed this scene, was convinced that Jazz had done his job. What would happen to Jazz and Amy now? What new disguise would Tyrone have to assume to penetrate the mob and bring down Mr. Anthony?

Tyrone, disguised as Leon Monroe, never took off the pendant that Amy had given him.

Cricket was the object of both Danny's and Phillip's affections, but it was Nina who walked away with the prize.

The summer of 1987 was a restless one for Genoa City's younger set, especially rock star Danny Romalotti; Jabot model Cricket Blair; and heir to the Chancellor millions, Phillip Chancellor III. Danny suggested to Cricket that they date others during the summer and reevaluate their relationship in the fall. Cricket took notice of painfully shy Phillip, who was greatly attracted to her but felt he couldn't measure up to Danny. With Katherine prodding him to date Cricket, Phillip secretly used alcohol to pump up his courage to pursue her. Before the summer was over, the two teenagers had shared so much that Phillip proposed, hoping Cricket would want to spend the rest of her life with him. Katherine and Jill, meanwhile, took time out from their battle over guardianship of Phillip to express their approval over the young lovers' betrothal. And Danny realized how much he truly loved Cricket, and regretted letting her go. He too proposed, hoping it was not too late for him, but Cricket chose Phillip. Then her roommate, Nina Webster, who had also set her sights on Phillip, came in for the kill and seduced him. Soon Nina announced she was expecting Phillip's child, and Cricket broke off her engagement to him, giving Danny new hope.

DANNY ▲ CRICKET ▲ PHILLIP

JILL ▲ REX ▲ KATHERINE

Rex Sterling found himself on a slippery slope when he married Jill after his divorce from Katherine (really Marge) came through. For Jill, who had arranged for the "old trout" to meet sexy Rexy in the first place, this was a huge mistake! Rex and Katherine (the real Katherine) had always gotten along famously—until Katherine (Marge again) suddenly began to act as if she had lost all her marbles. Despite his best efforts to bring his "wife" back to her senses, Katherine did whatever she wanted to do, and began selling the Chancellor estate and all her properties right from under Rex's nose. So Rex gave up on her and moved in with Jill, who helped him get a divorce and then married him herself. But Katherine (the real one) got the last laugh. She took advantage of a huge loophole which invalidated Jill's marriage to Rex. It took no time for Jill and Rex to two-time each other; once again Jill tried to get close to John Abbott, and Rex, posing as a guy named "Roger," tried to make points with Leanna Love. Then Katherine threw a big party, invited all the principles and enjoyed the fun of seeing them trying to cover their tracks.

Jill and her assistant, David Kimble, found a bum on a park bench and gave him the regal name of Rex Sterling. She immediately knew she had found the perfect romantic partner for Katherine Chancellor.

Rex was always able to reason with Katherine; their marriage was based on mutual love and respect.

After Katherine and Rex married, Rex became the mediator between the two bickering women.

Jill and Rex's marriage certificate.

After Katherine (really Marge) and Rex parted, Rex turned to Jill, who happily helped him with his divorce.

NIKKI ▲ VICTOR ▲ ASHLEY

Victor was caught in the middle between two beautiful women, exactly where he wanted to be.

Victor loved Nikki as he loved no other woman. But he also loved the intelligent and beautiful Ashley Abbott, whose ability to head a complex corporation astounded him. He was able to share with Ashley his plans and schemes of annexing even more power and greater wealth. Nikki, though, was not beyond using her wiles and cunning to hold on to Victor. Everything took second place—concerns over her personal health, the needs of their children—in Nikki's effort to make Victor jealous, and she wept buckets of tears and pushed all the right buttons to bring her husband home. But Ashley knew her way around Victor's heart as well and put up a good fight for his attention and affections, if at times merely to vex, confound or outdo Nikki. In the end it was Ashley's concern for others and her great sense of duty to family (hers as well as Victor's) that made her give up Victor.

Later in their relationship, Ryan cozied up to Nina, a situation covetous Victoria found hard to accept.

What a situation to find oneself in. Ryan McNeil was caught between two predatory women vying for his attention. On one side was the nubile but fragile 16-year-old Victoria Newman, and on the other, the slightly older Nina Chancellor, a gal with a past who'd been around the block a time or two. If the truth be known, Ryan relished the opportunity to teach Victoria a few tricks, while he anticipated learning a few tricks from Nina. Both young women were emotionally vulnerable, and both carried excess baggage. And Ryan had to figure in Victoria's awesome, hard-

nosed father, the tycoon Victor Newman, who'd be sure to hold Ryan accountable were he to harm a single hair on his precious one's head. Both women had plied him with extravagant graduation gifts—an expensive watch from Victoria and a shiny red convertible from Nina. They sat side by side at Ryan's commencement exercises, each talking about their "boyfriend," not knowing that they were speaking about the same person. This triangle flattened out when Ryan, who was engaged to Nina, married Victoria, only to later divorce Victoria and marry Nina.

Brad came home to find Traci talking
with her new editor, Steve Connelly.

BRAD ▲ TRACI ▲ STEVE

Traci couldn't quite put her finger on it, but there was
an elusive something missing in her marriage to Brad,
something so drastically wrong that it would drive her
into the arms of another man. Was it that Brad didn't
show her the respect she craved, and didn't regard her
as a person? As his equal? When Traci turned to writing as an escape, it seemed natural to write from the
heart. Her editor, Steve Connelly, instantly picked up
on it.

> STEVE: *The way you've involved me with your
> characters is quite extraordinary. That mo-
> ment when Lela confronts Tom about his
> ambivalence. You've turned her inside out.
> It's one of the most difficult things to cap-
> ture on the printed page. My hat's off to
> you, Traci.*

> TRACI: *I don't know what to say but thank-you.*

Traci found Steve to be simpatico.

Brad and Steve exchanged angry words over Traci and Brad's little daughter Colleen.

After Traci and Brad divorced, she married Steve, and they lived in New York with her daughter Colleen.

STEVE: *You know, to create a character like that, you've had to have known someone like Lela...watched her go through the same kind of turmoil...someone whose relationship to reality doesn't match up to her dream...*

Steve cut right to the chase. They talked endlessly about ways for Traci to strengthen her novel, her characters, her life. She became a different person that night. And Brad sensed that something was different about his wife: the way she looked, the way she spoke, the excitement in her voice when she talked about her novel. She started that very moment, and began a new chapter in her life. She had also fallen in love with Steve—the man who measured up to and understood her dreams.

Traci Abbott's first novel.

ECHOES OF THE PAST

DEBUT OF A NEW AUTHOR

TRACI ABBOTT

JILL ▴ JOHN ▴ MAMIE

For years, Mamie Johnson, the Abbott's loyal maid, kept her mouth shut, and her eyes fully open. With the exception of Jill, she was loved and trusted by all of the members of the Abbott family. So when Mamie began to suspect that Jill was involved with Jed Sanders, the home improvement man, she lost no time in confronting the lady of the house. The verbal warfare between the two soon escalated dramatically, for Mamie, who was falling in love with her boss, was not about to see him hurt by Jill. Jill, on the other hand, who was undeniably in love with John's wealth, dug into her own cache and paid Mamie a considerable sum of money on the condition that the maid take a permanent, well-deserved vacation.

The confrontations between John and Jill would be maid to order, if Mamie could have John all to herself.

A depressed Mamie could not accept the spirit of peace on earth, good will toward Jill in the face of Jill's carrying on with Jed Sanders.

Would the New Year signal a peaceful coexistence for all three?

DANNY ▲ CHRISTINE ▲ PAUL

Paul entered Christine's life after her marriage to Danny had ended. Their love grew out of a deep friendship based on sharing and understanding. Paul had been hurt by Lauren and Cassandra; and Christine, who had pledged to love Danny forever, found forever to be but a brief moment. Hardly a year after agreeing to a long-distance marriage—Danny in New York and she in Genoa City—Christine received a "Dear Christine" letter. Danny wrote that he had found someone else and wanted a divorce, which Christine, devastated by his betrayal, gave him. Paul then slowly, quietly, grew closer to Chris. When Danny returned, he wanted her back, claiming he had been tricked into marrying Phyllis. Relentless in his pursuit, he insisted he would divorce Phyllis; he claimed he never loved her. Christine, he said, was the true love of his life. Christine tried to shut Danny out, but the love they had shared never really died.

Paul stopped by to spend the evening with Chris and couldn't believe his eyes when he found his fiancée and Danny together.

Still, Christine said they would always be good friends, and she reluctantly counseled Danny as he tried to extricate himself from his marriage. When all of these efforts failed, Danny went to Christine for a sympathetic shoulder. She comforted him a little too much; they both got caught up in the moment and made love. When Paul stopped over that evening to see his fiancée, he couldn't believe his eyes. He later confronted Christine, called off their wedding and punched out Danny.

Paul wanted to marry Chris. Danny was hoping to win her back.

MOST MEMORABLE
Friendships and Rivalries

There are friendships, and then there are friendships. *There's the straight-from-the-heart kind which one human being extends to another—no strings attached, with little expected in return. It's the kind a Cricket extends to a Nina, or a Brock Reynolds or a Rex Sterling to whomever would have been lucky enough to be on the receiving end of their generous, missionary-like, selfless selves. Some friendships turn into romantic partnerships, some stop a mite short.*

Then there are rivalries and there are rivalries. *There's the kind that seems to go on forever, such as those between Jill and Katherine, Jack and Victor and Lauren and Traci. Many families in real life are breeding grounds for rivalries between siblings such as those between Jack and Ashley Abbott or between Leslie and Lorie Brooks. Sometimes, hard-core rivals may call a temporary truce, as Jill and Katherine occasionally did. Jeanne Cooper (Katherine) described it thusly, "That's the love/hate thing: I hate you so much I wouldn't want to lose you because I wouldn't have anyone that I love so much to hate."*

Finally, there's the alliance that has the potential for straddling the line. We call it the "friendship" of convenience, like the union of Brad Carlton and Jack Abbott, which is invariably for mutual gain. This union is the scary kind, because it can go either way. You never know what to expect.

SNAPPER AND CASEY

Casey and Snapper were not only colleagues, but also good friends.

Snapper Foster was captivated by his colleague Dr. Casey Reed's brilliance; he was not used to seeing women doctors in action. Snapper was also in the midst of his own private pain—his wife Chris had left him "to find herself" in the wake of losing her battle to adopt little Karen Becker. Lonely and despairing, Snapper decided to move into the resident quarters of the hospital and, as luck would have it, Casey occupied the room adjoining his. Casey made it clear from the beginning that she had no intention of getting involved with him, and Snapper admired her honesty and directness. He later learned that Casey's father had tempered her feelings toward men; he had mistreated Casey's mother and had raped Casey when she was a teenager. Snapper's heart went out to her and he swore he would do anything to show her that all men were not like her father. He won Casey's admiration and friendship when he helped steer her rebellious younger sister, Nikki, toward a safer, healthier lifestyle. Snapper finally confessed his feelings to Casey, but a phone call from Chris kept him from pursuing it further, and he immediately returned home to be with his wife, who made no demands on him. Later, Casey confessed that she trusted Snapper completely and she was ready to let nature take its course. But Snapper backed away. Chris, in turn, realized how close she had come to losing her husband. Casey urged Snapper to not give up on his marriage. As for her, thanks to Snapper's loving friendship, she'd become better able to deal with the cards life had handed her.

KATHERINE AND JOANN

Although the pattern of taking young women into her home had been set by Katherine some few years earlier when she took in Jill Foster, this time it was different. For, this time, Katherine was not the initiator when she agreed to hire the unhappy, oversized woman as her paid companion. Rather, it was her son Brock who persuaded his reluctant mother to give it a go, pointing out that the commonality of their loneliness would bridge the wide differences in their ages and temperaments. Joann, it seems, had been eating compulsively ever since her husband, Professor Jack Curtis (Johnny to her), divorced her because she was not the same attractive, shapely young woman he had married. In fact, he was now heavily involved with Peggy Brooks, whom he had romanced while still married to Joann, neglecting to tell her, of course, that he had a wife. He would soon marry Peggy, putting his relationship with Joann completely in his past. With the zeal of a missionary, Katherine was determined to save Joann, body and soul. Before too long, she had transformed Joann back into her slender, attractive self, only this time clad in beautiful and expensive clothes. But Joann was still having difficulty getting Johnny out of her system. No man was worth it, Katherine told Joann, and neither was making new friends, because it would just open her up to new hurts. Brock didn't like what he was witnessing. He knew his mother wanted to possess Joann; her love had become smothering. So Brock sat "The Duchess" down and talked cold turkey to her. Then, lucky for both Katherine and Joann, Derek Thurston walked into Katherine's life, giving her a new mission. Painful as it was, Katherine kicked Joann out, but not before offering her a job managing Derek's soon-to-open styling salon. Katherine pointed out that Joann's great weight loss would be an inspiration to their clients.

After Joann Curtis had gained an enormous amount of weight and Johnny had left her, she turned to Katherine for friendship and support.

At first, Katherine's son Brock encouraged his mother's friendship with Joann, but he later questioned it when she became too zealous.

KATHERINE AND FELIPE

Katherine had all she needed in her new, simple life in Jamaica: the sun, the sea, the fish, the bananas...and her dear friend, Felipe.

It was one of the most unlikely alliances either of them could have imagined; a fateful encounter that blossomed into a friendship that would change both of their lives. She, the wealthy Katherine Chancellor Thurston, despondent over her scam of a marriage to Derek, jumped overboard while on a "second honeymoon" cruise Derek had arranged to try to keep his job at Chancellor Industries. Life just wasn't worth living. He, Felipe Ramirez, a Cuban revolutionary hiding from the authorities in Jamaica, rescued Katherine and saved her life. But Felipe refused to take her back to her world. He hated people of wealth, and if she wanted to go back, she'd have to get there herself. But they could help each other, Felipe said. She could help him improve his English, and he could put her to work on the island—fishing, cleaning, cooking—to help break her dependence on the bottle. It worked for a while, and Katherine and Felipe grew close. She adjusted to the simple life, content to leave her past behind. But it was not to be.

Katherine suffered a severe cut on her foot, which became infected and threatened her life. Convinced she would die—everyone back home already thought she was dead—Katherine expressed her deep friendship for Felipe, wishing he had come into her life long ago. To show her gratitude, she would arrange for her lawyers to draw up counterfeit papers so he could go to the States to live. The lawyers would also see to it that his political writings would be published.

As Katherine's condition worsened, Felipe was determined to return her to civilization and the medical attention she desperately needed. He gently placed her in his boat and headed for Montego Bay, risking his own life in the process were he to be discovered. At the hospital, Katherine was administered last rites, but then began a miraculous recovery. Meanwhile, Douglas Austin, who had flown to Montego Bay to search for Katherine, professed his love for her to Felipe, saying he planned to take her back to Genoa City and marry her. When Felipe realized Katherine would be taken care of, he penned a good-bye letter and left. Recovered, Katherine announced plans to stay in Jamaica and find Felipe, the first man she ever truly respected, the man who taught her so much about truth, so much about herself. She didn't need Derek, or Douglas for that matter. Tragically, Katherine learned Felipe's boat was bombed, and blamed herself for his death. If it hadn't been for his coming out of hiding to get her to the hospital, Felipe would still be alive. Much to her surprise and joy, when Katherine wandered back to Felipe's hut, she found him alive! She wanted to stay with him on the island, but he knew she would be happier in her own world, and he had his political work that needed to be done. If it was meant to be, he said, they'd meet up again some day, the fates would see to it. So with the newfound strength and resolve that she drew from this extraordinary man, Katherine returned to Genoa City to begin her life anew.

CRICKET AND NINA

Cricket and Nina's friendship began when they were both teenagers. Cricket helped Nina put her past behind her and look toward a happy future.

Nina was unmarried, pregnant and alone when Cricket took her in and befriended her.

"I was alone again and on the streets...except for Cricket. She was there for me during the hardest time of my life. I honestly don't think I would've survived if it hadn't been for her."

Cricket Blair befriended Nina Webster and gave her a place to live when she was a lonely, pregnant teenager. Cricket tried to tolerate Nina's ruffian ways, but threw her out more than once for lying and for stealing (not only money, but her boyfriend, Phillip). Their relationship worked, though, because Cricket needed to be needed, and there was no one more in need of a friend than Nina. When Nina gave birth to young Phillip Chancellor's son, she begged Cricket to be a mother to her baby if she should die. And when Cricket realized that Phillip would always carry the baggage of Nina and the baby, she stepped aside and helped Nina win Phillip's heart. She was even there to pick up the pieces when Phillip self-destructed. The two friends survived their teens, Nina later becoming the strong one for Cricket, helping her friend through her share of difficult times. Their friendship not only withstood the test of time, but grew stronger over the years. No matter what the crisis, or how difficult the dilemma, Nina and Cricket would get through it together, each with the other's support. And when it was time to celebrate and share happy times, they did that together, too. Through it all, they've always been, and will always be, the best of friends.

VICTOR AND DOUGLAS

If Victor Newman really had placed this ad, only one person would've been qualified for the job: Douglas Austin. These two had a long history together. Douglas would do everything in his power—legal or otherwise—to help Victor accomplish whatever Victor wanted to accomplish. At every critical moment in Victor's life, Douglas was there for his friend. He knew what was good for Victor and he knew what was bad for Victor. And Victor, surprisingly, usually heeded Douglas's advice.

Douglas left his friend Victor after many years, returning to England to tend to a family crisis that needed his attention.

Douglas Austin (the Colonel) was Victor Newman's confidant, co-conspirator and more than once, best man (here, celebrating Victor's marriage to Hope).

PAUL AND LYNNE

As secretary for Paul Williams Investigations, Lynne Bassett couldn't have been more efficient or more loyal. Lynne was also one of the truest friends Paul ever had. She could read Paul's moods better than anyone, and was always there to lend an understanding ear. Lynne kept a close watch on Paul's love life, hoping someday he might realize that she was the woman for him. They did test the waters a few times—romantic dinners and a ski trip—but the sparks just never flew for Paul. His mother tried her best to coax them closer; she saw Lynne as the perfect match for her unlucky-in-love son. Lynne finally confessed her love to Paul, but she was a good enough friend to put his feelings first, realized it wasn't meant to be and tried to get him to reconcile with his true love, Chris. Lynne would always love Paul, and still, in a small corner of her heart, hoped he might return that love. Paul could only hope he wouldn't break her heart again. He knew he could never ask for a better friend than Lynne.

Lynne was always there for Paul, manning the phones, taking care of business and lending a friendly ear.

Paul gave Lynne money to buy an evening gown; then, as reward for her loyal service, he took her out for a night on the town. Lynne hoped it would turn into something more.

MALCOLM AND KEESHA

With Malcolm, Keesha Monroe experienced the best that friendship had to offer. When the rest of the world cast her aside and AIDS was draining the life from her frail body, Malcolm risked the relationship he was so desperate to build with his family to be by her side. In a moment of true selflessness, he gave her one final, special gift. Only minutes before she died, they became husband and wife in a simple ceremony in her apartment.

REVEREND GREER: *God has given us life. It is a miracle we enjoy as best we can for what time we are given to enjoy it. No man or woman can tell how long the thread of life will be.*

Try as we may, though, life sometimes seems harsh, unfair, unfeeling. We seek answers we cannot find. We seek to understand what cannot be understood. There is pain, confusion, and loss we sometimes find unbearable. For this reason, God, in His infinite goodness, has given us a balm for our souls. That balm is love.

Today, Malcolm and Keesha have chosen to enter into a perfect and timeless expression of their love for one another by joining in marriage.

Malcolm, do you take this woman to be your wife? Will you shelter her? Make a safe place for her in your heart? Will you give her without condition or restraint that best part of yourself, marrying your soul to hers so that wherever she may go, she may always find warmth and comfort and the knowledge that she is not alone? Will you bring light to her life by accepting that which is best in her—the love she gives to you?

MALCOLM: *Oh, yes. I will.*
Keesha, I am your husband.

(MALCOLM LIFTS HER VEIL,
LEANS IN SLOWLY AND GENTLY, AND KISSES HER)

Left: Malcolm and Keesha were attracted to one another, but couldn't begin to understand the troubles that lay ahead.

Right: Malcolm surprised Keesha with an at-home picnic early in their relationship. Later, when she battled AIDS, he would nourish her with food and companionship.

Keesha had lost everything, but Malcolm knew he could bring his friend one more moment of happiness before she died.

Jill loved living in the Chancellor mansion, where she tended to Katherine's whims and needs.

KATHERINE AND JILL

Katherine Chancellor Sterling vs. Jill Foster Abbott. One of soap operadom's longest-running feuds (23 years) was fought over the many men these two women shared. It all began when socialite Katherine Chancellor accused impoverished Jill of seducing her husband. To save her marriage, Katherine talked her only son, Brock Reynolds, who was already attracted to Jill, into a marriage with her, which ended when Jill discovered she was pregnant with Phillip's child. The next man to come into their lives was handsome cosmetologist Derek Thurston, who had big dreams. Jill saw and fell in love with him first, but it was Katherine who married him, using her wealth as bait. When that marriage ended in divorce, debonair Rex Sterling, whom Jill had set up to date Katherine as a prank, became Katherine's next husband. By this time, Jill had set her own sights on capturing Katherine's good friend, John Abbott. Employing every trick in her arsenal to thwart this marriage, Katherine confronted John and used his ex-wife Dina, loyal maid Mamie and the entire Abbott clan to gang up on him. But John wouldn't listen, and he went ahead and married Jill anyway. Katherine watched Jill like a hawk and, when John's son Jack had a dalliance with her, Katherine came up with photographic evidence of the indiscretion and gleefully presented it to John. That marriage was over.

Katherine and Phillip in happier days.

Although neither Jill nor Phillip wanted it to happen, they fell in love.

But when Katherine had a bit of hard luck herself and divorced Rex, Jill married him. Not to be outdone, Katherine had the marriage declared invalid. Jill ultimately remarried John Abbott, again to the consternation of Katherine, Mamie and the Abbott kids. But the union once again collapsed, and it wasn't long before the feud between Katherine and Jill became physical. When Katherine duped Jill into believing she was going to testify on her behalf in her custody battle with John over little Billy, the two ladies had a vicious catfight in the courtroom corridor.

Katherine and Jill acting out their "endearments."

If there was any single moment in their stormy relationship that was completely out of character, it was when Jill called a truce because of Katherine's breast cancer scare. Jill was actually there for Katherine, acting as her confidante and offering comfort. However, once Katherine received a clean bill of health, the two were at it again, and the fussing, feuding and fighting continues to this day.

About Katherine and Jill's rivalry, which has gone on since 1973, Jeanne Cooper said, "That's an ongoing miracle of sorts...the fact that these two—one or the other—has not killed one or the other."

Victor was Jack's nemesis, not only in business, but also where Nikki and Ashley were concerned.

VICTOR AND JACK

There are no greater rivals in this world than Victor Newman and Jack Abbott. The battle lines were drawn a long time ago and run deep into their souls. Ashley. Nikki. Jabot. Ashley Abbott, Jack's sister, was Victor's confidante and later his wife. Jack contended that Victor brought Ashley nothing but heartache and unhappiness. Nikki Newman Abbott. Her name says it all. Whether married to her or not, Victor saw Nikki as his. And Jack had the audacity to marry her! For years, Victor and Jack vied for control of Jabot, the company Jack's father, John Abbott, built singlehandedly from the ground up. Each was convinced he was the better man for the job, and they'd stop at nothing to have it their way, hopefully at great expense to the other. When Jack lost the company to Victor, he did the unthinkable: he accepted an offer from Victor that meant abandoning Nikki and the children. In return, control of Jabot would return to the Abbotts. Furious with both men, Nikki wondered how far Victor would go to manipulate her. How could Jack even consider using his wife and family as a pawn in a business deal? With the document signed and delivered, Jack was certain Jabot would be returned to its rightful owners. But time had run out before the document was signed, so Jack found himself desperately seeking not only the company, but also revenge on Victor. A few years later, Jack finally had the opportunity for the sweetest of revenges when he set a plan in motion to take over Newman Enterprises. But he didn't bank on getting caught in the act.

MAY 08, 1990
GENOA CITY, WISC.

THIS AGREEMENT HAS BEEN ENTERED INTO BY VICTOR NEWMAN
AND JACK ABBOTT ON TUESDAY, MAY 8TH, 1990. THE TERMS ARE AS FOLLOWS:

I, VICTOR NEWMAN, AGREE TO GIVE UP CONTROL OF JABOT COSMETICS,
AND RETURN MY HOLDINGS AND INTERESTS IN SAID COMPANY, TO THE ABBOTT
FAMILY.

IN RETURN, I, JACK ABBOTT AGREE TO ABANDON MY WIFE, NIKKI REED NEWMAN,
AND NEVER COME NEAR HER CHILDREN AGAIN. UNLESS THIS AGREEMENT IS
SIGNED WITHIN TWENTY-FOUR HOURS, IT BECOMES NULL AND VOID.

_____
SIGNED_____
        JACK ABBOTT
SIGNED_____
        VICTOR NEWMAN   ON THIS
WITNESSED_____
        DAY OF MAY, 1990. AT_____O'CLOCK.

Both Jack and Victor signed this agreement, but a legal loophole left Victor still in control, and Jack out in the cold.

Jack had to get past Victor to return his father's company to Abbott family control.

Victor Newman had the greatest respect for John Abbott, a self-made man like himself. It was John's son, Jack, whom Victor couldn't stand.

VICTOR: *I consider this mutiny, Abbott. Out and out betrayal. You were clearly making a power play! Intending to use this time while I'm away to usurp me. Well, it is not going to happen! Do you understand?! Not now, not ever. Go back to your office...pack your things...and get the hell out! I never want to see your face again! You were only tolerated this long because of your sister and your father. You've always been a devious man...but this time you've gone too far! You will regret for the rest of your life that you ever tried to take me on! I can't tell you how much pleasure it gives me to be rid of you, Jack Abbott! You are the most despicable, unsavory human being I've ever had the misfortune to...*

That was as far as Victor got before he collapsed. Jack's immediate reaction was to help Victor, but he hesitated and looked at his rival for a long moment. Then Jack left Victor to die. But his conscience made him return to the office and he called the paramedics. Victor survived the ordeal and the battle royale between Jack and Victor continued.

Genoa City Chronicle ☆ ☆ BUSINESS SECTION

Jack Abbott to Succeed Victor Newman

JACK ABBOTT   BRADLEY CARLTON

Peter Bergman described the scene when Victor was stricken: "I walked. I not only walked, I stepped over the body. I not only stepped over the body, but in the process of going out, without meaning to, I kicked his hand! And I was so glad they got it on camera! It was this tiny little moment, but it was insult to injury. The blow on the bruise. It was a kind of final statement....And I remember seeing it on the screen and thinking, what a delicious moment! What a really, really swell moment!"

Knowing that Traci would have a hard time resisting the banana split she had ordered for her, Lauren sat back to enjoy the fun. Traci decided to return the split. "It's on you," she said.

TRACI AND LAUREN

Shy Traci Abbott was extremely sensitive about her weight. Extroverted Lauren Fenmore flaunted her shapely figure. But the two were evenly matched when it came to playing dirty tricks on each other. In the summer of 1983, they competed for the attention of rock star Danny Romalotti. Traci was on a strict diet and exercise regimen. While studying one day in the campus coffee shop, she could not help but notice Lauren's grand entrance on Danny's arm. Once Danny left the coffee shop, Lauren had a giant banana split sent over to Traci's table. Dying to eat it, Traci instead marched over to Lauren's table and returned the confection, coolly dumping it over Lauren's head! This, however, did not prevent Lauren from eating humble pie when she needed Traci's help to pass the English exam. Lauren offered a pizza to Traci, the conscientious superstudent, if she could borrow Traci's notes. Tempted to refuse, Traci spelled out the terms: return the notes at least two hours before the exam so that she would have one last chance to review them. True to form, Lauren returned the notes to the exasperated Traci just twenty minutes before the exam, but Traci carefully watched Lauren's reaction as it dawned on Lauren that Traci had given her the wrong notes to study!

Danny Romalotti was putty in the hands of gorgeous, manipulative Lauren Fenmore.

But the time when Traci was to sing at Danny's concert was priceless. Jealous Lauren slipped a "Mickey" into Traci's iced tea, intending to step in for her "dear friend" after Traci keeled over. The plan backfired, though, when the drinks were switched by Traci's pals. Lauren collapsed, while Traci captivated the audience—and Danny—with her singing. Both women eventually got over Danny, but their rivalry continued into their adult years.

Ten years later, Traci was divorced from Brad Carlton and living in New York City with her daughter, Colleen, and her new husband, publisher Steve Connelly. Lauren, meanwhile, had been dating Brad, who suffered a near-fatal heart attack in her bed. It was Lauren who broke the news to Traci, and she immediately returned to Genoa City to be with her ex-husband. When she found out, though, that this happened in Lauren's bed, it was more than Traci could bear, and she dove for Lauren. It took an orderly and a nurse to pull the two apart.

When another one of Lauren's mean tricks backfired, Traci triumphantly performed with her idol, Danny Romalotti.

For years the two women fought over their men, and here Lauren put a damper on Traci's plan to emerge victorious.

An orderly and a nurse broke up the fight. Stunt doubles played the combatants.

As she was growing up, shy Leslie Brooks spent countless hours practicing the piano.

LORIE AND LESLIE

From childhood, fragile, shy, insecure Leslie Brooks practiced the piano morning, noon and night, preparing for the brilliant concert career she prayed would one day be hers. She got much of her parents' attention and was deeply resented by her younger sister Lorie. And so it was that with each passing year, the chasm between the two sisters widened, with Lorie scheming and counting the ways to even the score. First there was handsome Brad Eliot, adored by Leslie and adoring her in return, spending countless hours with her, encouraging her and bringing her out of her shell to face the demands of her career. Somehow, Lorie had managed to convince Leslie that Brad was losing interest in her and Brad into accepting that Leslie no longer had time for him. The stage was set for the opening night of Leslie's all-important concert series. Her brilliant career was nearing its zenith, but Lorie led Leslie to believe that even as she played, Brad would be in her bed, making love to her! With her hands in midair, poised above the keyboard, that image flashed through Leslie's mind, and she entered into a state of complete paralysis. She didn't remember a thing—not leaving the stage or her nervous collapse or the months of institutionalization. Nothing! It was all one big blank.

But Lorie was right there when Leslie recovered for an encore performance. This time, Lorie flaunted her love affair with Lance Prentiss, the love of Leslie's life. Then, under the pseudonym S.M. Brand, Lorie wrote her bestselling, autobiographical novel, *In My Sister's Shadow*, revealing all the dirt behind an "acclaimed concert pianist's nervous breakdown," causing Leslie to once again relive the pain and anguish. Somehow, Lorie always managed to reduce to insignificance the accolades Leslie received from her adoring public, but their father's attention to Leslie would forever be a stake, piercing Lorie's evil, jealous heart.

Wherever she played as a brilliant concert pianist, Leslie was hailed.

The typewriter was the instrument Leslie's cunning sister Lorie used to document the resentment she felt living *In My Sister's Shadow*.

THE ABBOTT SIBLINGS

Jack and Ashley couldn't agree on how to treat their mother, Dina Abbott Mergeron.

Just your typical sibling relationships: a brother and two sisters who occasionally fought and occasionally made peace. But since they were the children of Genoa City's prominent Abbott clan, the stakes were higher than for most brother and sister feuds. There were two distinct rivalries: Jack and his oldest sister, Ashley; and Ashley and her baby sister, Traci. For bad boy Jack and wise-beyond-her-years Ashley, the rivalry stemmed from their jockeying for the presidency of the family business, Jabot Cosmetics. Jack lost the job to Ashley when he got shot; Ashley lost it to Jack when he blackmailed her and threatened to reveal her true parentage. Ashley had no recourse. She stepped down and Jack again took control. Ashley later married Victor and was heir apparent to Newman Enterprises, but when Victor "died," Jack just assumed the head honcho's job would be his. Despite their business rivalry, Jack and Ashley came to love each other dearly. Family crises had a way of bringing them together, especially where John's health was concerned. But when it came to other matters of John's heart (like their mother, Dina), the siblings clashed again. Jack, it seemed, was much quicker to forgive and forget than Ashley.

As for the other sibling duo, Ashley and Traci, Brad Carlton was the force that came between them. It didn't help matters that Ashley was a natural beauty. Insecure Traci was more than a little jealous of her sister, and always imagined the worst as far as Ashley and Brad's friendship was concerned. Their sisterly love was truly tested when Ashley and Brad were almost engaged before Traci returned from New York—but Ashley married Victor instead, leaving Traci and Brad to remarry and start a family.

The Abbott children had their share of sibling quarrels: Jack and Ashley over business; Ashley and Traci over Brad.

JACK AND BRAD

Jack wanted to head up Newman Enterprises, and had a difficult time accepting "Golden Boy" Brad's meteoric rise from pool boy to corporate exec.

Jack Abbott and Brad Carlton fought over the president's seat at Newman Enterprises. Brad couldn't stand the thought of having to answer to Jack at work. Jack found the thought of "Bradsky" as his boss equally revolting. Jack also hated that Brad came between his sisters, Ashley and Traci, and Brad blamed Jack for putting Traci smack in the middle of their business affairs. The fact that they agreed on Victor's neglect of Newman Enterprises should have brought them eye to eye, but they instead found themselves head to head in a battle over who would succeed Victor at the helm following Victor's "death." Jack would assume as CEO. After Victor's stunning return, the rivals continued their bickering, and at various times, each joined forces with Victor to fight the other.

PAUL AND BRAD

There was no love lost between Brad Carlton and Paul Williams when it came to Cassandra Rawlins. Cassandra was the love of Paul's life. When they separated, Cassandra took an interest in Brad for more than his business acumen. Both men were curious about the others' state of involvement with Ms. Rawlins, but it was Paul who was stung when Cassandra and Brad wed. The newspaper account of Brad and Cassandra's divorce only a few weeks later was enough to send the usually levelheaded detective into a rage; he'd fight to the end with Carlton or anyone else to protect Cassandra's honor. His devotion paid off when Cassie left him her fortune, but he and Brad came to blows again over who was the rightful heir. Brad and Cassandra, it seemed, were never officially divorced, so Brad laid legal claim to the estate.

Paul and Brad argued more than
once over the same woman:
Cassandra Rawlins.

Fisticuffs flew over Paul's refusal
to let Brad's actions tarnish
Cassandra's image.

Families

When "The Young and the Restless" first began, the core families were the rich Brookses, the poor but ascending Fosters and the Chancellors (now the Chancellor/Sterlings). Ten years later they were replaced by the moderately wealthy Abbotts, the obscenely wealthy Newmans and the middle-class Williamses. More recently, two new and exciting families have been added to the mix: the Hastings and the Winters. Family has always been the centerpiece of soap operas. There are rich families who are poor and poor families who are rich. There are siblings who could destroy each other without a second thought and there are siblings who would lay down their lives for each other. There are good parents, there are rotten parents, and there are good children and evil children. And wouldn't you know it, they're all in Genoa City!

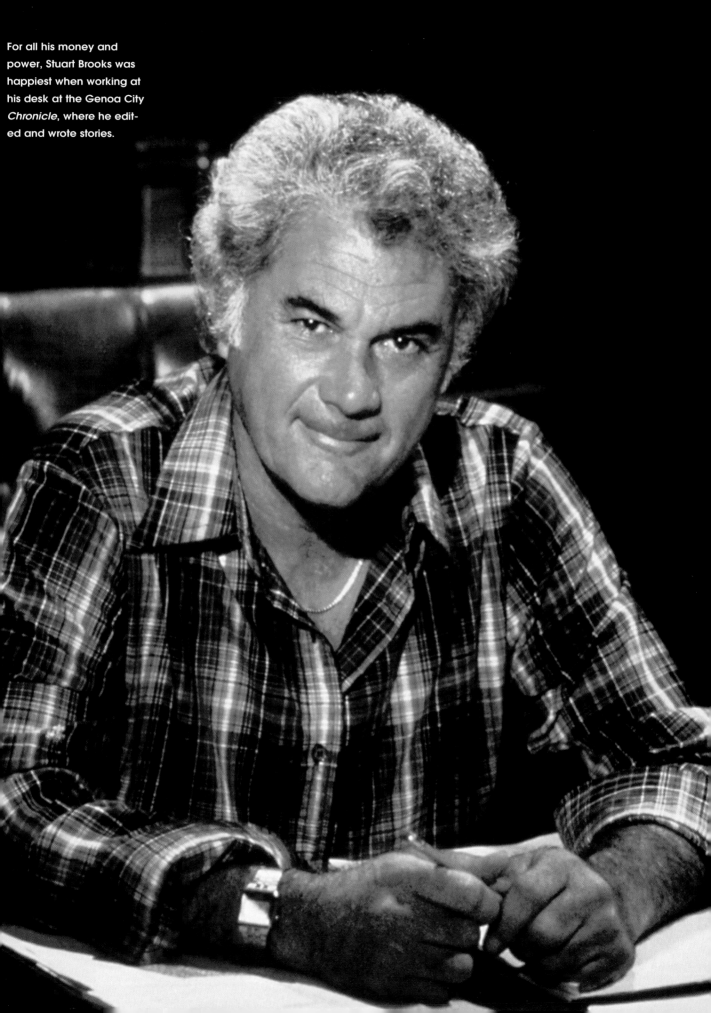

For all his money and power, Stuart Brooks was happiest when working at his desk at the Genoa City *Chronicle*, where he edited and wrote stories.

THE BROOKS

When "The Young and the Restless" premiered, the Brooks family was one of the most outstanding families in Genoa City. Newspaper publisher Stuart Brooks and his wife Jennifer were the parents of four beautiful daughters: Leslie, Lorie, Chris, and Peggy. Jennifer and Stuart loved their daughters equally and tried to help them in every way possible. Stuart, especially, spent quality time nurturing them, encouraging each to become everything she was capable of being. Leslie became an acclaimed concert pianist; Lorie, a best-selling novelist; and younger daughter Peggy, an accomplished journalist. Daughter Chris, who wanted more than anything to marry at an early age and raise a family, married Dr. Snapper Foster and raised a daughter.

But for all of Stuart's concern for his daughters' happiness, after many seemingly happy years into his own marriage to Jennifer, he was shocked to learn of his wife's long-past affair with an old flame. And he never suspected that the high-spirited Lorie was not his own child. Stuart, however, forgave Jennifer and after she died, he found a second chance at happiness when he married Liz Foster, his son-in-law's mother.

Stuart spent many hours encouraging Leslie to play the piano.

Stuart also devoted much time to his youngest daughter, Peggy, who wanted to be a journalist.

The Brooks sisters and Jennifer wished Leslie happiness as she prepared to marry Brad.

Stuart told his daughter Leslie how happy he was that she was marrying fine, upstanding Brad Eliot.

Older sister Chris always made time to listen to Peggy's problems and encouraged her to face life with directness and honesty.

Lorie Brooks missed many of the family gatherings because she was busy jetting all over the continent doing research for her first novel.

Jennifer gave Leslie some motherly advice as Leslie prepared for her marriage.

Leslie with her son, Brooks.

THE FOSTERS

Barely hanging in there could well describe the Fosters—Liz and her three children: William Jr. (Snapper), Greg and Jill. William Foster Sr. had run out on his family and left his wife the daunting task of raising their children as a single mother. Liz tried to instill high moral values in her children, who would do anything they could to relieve their mother from her dreary factory job. Liz also supplemented her income by doing housework for Katherine Chancellor. While Snapper went to medical school and his younger brother studied law, Jill helped out by working in a beauty salon. Snapper, who deeply resented his father's abandonment, paid his tuition by working part-time. He met and fell in love with Chris Brooks, a member of one of Genoa City's most prominent families. Chris's father, Stuart Brooks, took an immediate dislike to Snapper when he learned that the young man was seeing another woman, Sally Crawford, who later bore Snapper's son, Chuckie. Snapper eventually married Chris, and with his father-in-law's help through the difficult financial times, he finished medical school. Greg earned his law degree and put in many grueling hours establishing his practice. Their sister, Jill, also improved herself: she moved on from her job in the beauty salon to the Chancellor mansion, where she worked as a paid companion for Katherine.

Liz was grateful to Jill for helping put Snapper and Greg through school.

Greg and his mother engaged in earnest conversation regarding Bill Foster, who had just returned to his family.

On Liz's wedding day, Jill offered her mother some advice.

Liz and Bill recited their wedding vows while Snapper and Chris looked on.

Just when Elizabeth found happiness with a nice man named Sam Powers, her errant husband showed up, broke and terminally ill. Doing the right thing, the Fosters took Bill in and tried to make the time he had remaining as comfortable as they could; he and Liz remarried, and the children forgave him. Liz remained at his side when he was near death in the hospital, and she committed the ultimate act, pulling the plug on his life support system.

Because they didn't have much money, the Fosters had few pictures in their family album. They carried the things that meant the most to them in their hearts.

Snapper congratulated his parents on their remarriage.

As soon as he learned that Sally's son was his, Snapper did the honorable thing and told Chris. Years later, Sally decided to marry an old boyfriend. Here Snapper bids a tearful good-bye to his son, Chuckie.

THE CHANCELLOR/STERLINGS

Katherine Chancellor Sterling slowly turned the pages of the family photo album. It had been such a long time since she had looked at it.

Good thing neither Christine nor Danny nor Gina are here to see how emotional I've become. But Brock... wouldn't he say he always knew I had a heart? After all, I do have a reputation to protect. Strong. Resilient. I'm a survivor. Mustn't show sentimentality...

As Katherine continued to turn the pages, she recalled those early days with her husband Phillip, when he was so adept at running Chancellor Industries and made it seem so easy.

My son Brock. The really good thing that came out of my first marriage. You were my strength, Brock, so many times. You helped me much more than I helped you.

A blank check from Chancellor Industries! Must make sure no one signs this.

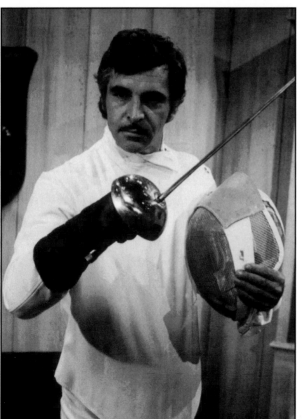

Ah, here's a photo of dear Phillip in his fencing gear. He was so accomplished....He loved sports. He loved to be challenged.

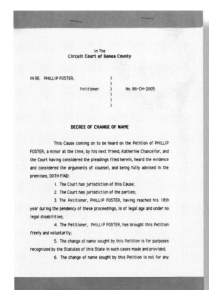

In The
Circuit Court of Genoa County

IN RE: PHILLIP FOSTER,   )
)
                Petitioner.   )   No. 86-CH-2005
)
)
)

DECREE OF CHANGE OF NAME

This Cause coming on to be heard on the Petition of PHILLIP
FOSTER, a minor at the time, by his next friend, Katherine Chancellor, and
the Court having considered the pleadings filed herein, heard the evidence
and considered the arguments of counsel, and being fully advised in the
premises, DOTH FIND:
    1. The Court has jurisdiction of this Cause;
    2. The Court has jurisdiction of the parties;
    3. The Petitioner, PHILLIP FOSTER, having reached his 18th
year during the pendency of these proceedings, is of legal age and under no
legal disabilities;
    4. The Petitioner, PHILLIP FOSTER, has brought this Petition
freely and voluntarily;
    5. The change of name sought by this Petition is for purposes
recognized by the Statutes of this State in such cases made and provided;
    6. The change of name sought by this Petition is not for any

What do we have here? The certificate for Phillip III's name change. My Phillip's son. We won't mention that tart, Jill Foster. How delicious that young Phillip decided to change his name from Foster to Chancellor! Oh how that bugged Jill!

Nina and her son, little Phillip. How his daddy would've loved him! Precious, precious boy!

Our Christmas parties were fun, weren't they? Sweet Rex, my husband. He was so good I married him twice! And his two loving children, Danny and Gina.

A dinner invitation. One of many, many, many such invites we used to send out. We did it all the time....I must have Danny and Gina come to dinner. And I must get Brock to come home to see his mother more often!

You Are Invited to
Dinner
on October 11th at 8 o'clock
at Katherine Chancellor
12 Foothill Road
Genoa City, Wisconsin
rsvp 555-

Cricket, I so wish you were still with Danny. But we did have happy times, didn't we?

I must've kept this picture even though that witch Jill's in it, because of Esther, Nina and John Silva.

Here's Esther and little Kate and me. I'm little Kate's godmother, you know! Which reminds me, where is that woman? Esther...put on a pot of coffee!

The Abbott family posed for a family portrait with their longtime maid, Mamie Johnson.

THE ABBOTTS

Today the Abbotts are one of Genoa City's core families. Headed by patriarch John Abbott, they are a tight family unit and want to keep it that way. Jack, the oldest son, and Ashley, the middle child, have, along with their father, made Jabot Cosmetics one of the premiere family-run cosmetics companies in the world. After years of struggling to find her direction and identity in life, Traci Carlton Connelly, the youngest, is now a successful novelist living in New York City with her publisher husband, Steve, and her small daughter, Colleen. Missing from the family unit was John's first wife, Dina, who abandoned the family some years ago. In the interim, John moved on with his life and had twice married Jill Foster, from whom he is now estranged. But Dina recently returned for a brief period, just long enough for John to rekindle his old feelings for her. She even moved closer to a reconciliation with Ashley, who, of her three children, found it the hardest to forgive her for having an extramarital affair with Brent Davis, Ashley's biological father.

John Abbott has always enjoyed having his grown children close by, whether living in the family home or staying there while visiting. And until a few years ago, the family was graced by the presence of live-in maid, Mamie Johnson, who was more of a mother to the Abbott siblings than the absentee Dina. The family enjoyed Mamie's cooking: mealtimes were the one time when they came together to catch up on the happenings of the day. As in every family, the Abbotts have had their disagreements and squabbles, but they always solve their problems in house and never flaunt their considerable wealth. The thorn in the Abbotts' side is John's estranged wife, Jill. Considerably younger than her husband and therefore hard to tame, as John Abbott puts it, Jill keeps the "old man" invigorated and gives him a passion for life. The two have a small son, Billy Foster Abbott, over whom they have battled for custody. A family such as the Abbotts has its moments, some big and some small, memories that will invariably last a lifetime.

It was truly a memorable moment when John's first wife, Dina Abbott Mergeron, paid a surprise visit to the Abbott home after an absence of many years.

Jack deeply loves his sisters Ashley and Traci.

Jack often played the role of friend and counselor to Traci, the most vulnerable of the Abbott siblings. Here he advised her on her writing career and her closeness to Steve Connelly, which was jeopardizing her marriage to Bradley Carlton.

Dina returned home for Traci's second wedding to Brad Carlton. John Abbott was happy for his youngest daughter.

The Abbott family came together for John's wedding to Cricket Blair's mother, Jessica. Pictured are (left to right): Steven Lassiter and his wife, Ashley; Danny Romalotti and Cricket; Jessica and John; Jack Abbott; Mamie; and Traci and her husband, Brad Carlton.

John and Jack have had their disagreements concerning family business matters, but Jack was always ready to give his utmost to Jabot.

Brent Davis is Ashley's biological father. She was conceived during his affair with her mother, Dina.

Jack and Ashley waited anxiously in the hospital where John had been rushed after a severe stroke.

Jack had a serious discussion with his stepmother, Jill Foster Abbott. The two dated before she married his father.

Jack Abbott held his stepbrother, little Billy Foster Abbott, while Jack's Vietnamese wife, Luan, stood by his side. They're discussing Jill's outrageous behavior with Mamie.

Of the John and Jill relationship, Jerry Douglas said, "I think that John loves her—that he's always loved her. She's brought out the youth in him and has made him a much younger man than he ever would have been. She's brought a lot of fun into his life."

The Abbotts—
John, Jill and lit-
tle Billy, sent this
happy holiday
greeting.

The Abbott clan gathered for Billy's
second birthday. Front row: John,
Billy, Mamie and Ashley. Second
row: Jack, Luan and Luan's two children, Mai and Keemo.

THE WILLIAMS

Mary and Carl Williams have four children: Steven, Paul, Patty and Todd. Their youngest son, Todd, is a priest in Europe. Steve and Patty, who lived in Genoa City at one time, have moved away. Steve moved to Washington, D.C., where he works on a newspaper, and Patty left town after her ill-fated marriage to Jack Abbott. Nice guy Paul operates a private detective agency and although he had many loves in his more youthful days, the present love of his life, Christine Blair, is his greatest love of all, and it seems destined to last forever.

Paul and his father have worked together on many investigative assignments, and Paul has had to go undercover a number of times, leading his mother, Mary, to believe more than once that her son was dead. It tore at Paul to do this to his mother. One time, when she was seriously ill and lay sleeping in her hospital bed, Paul had to sneak into her room in the middle of the night to see her. He whispered, "I love you, Mom," and then quickly left. The Williamses are a solid example of the typical middle-class American family. They have shared many memorable big and small moments.

A young Paul and his sister, Patty, horsed around.

Mary Williams had a habit of intruding upon intimate scenes. She greatly disapproved of Lauren Fenmore.

Paul was always working
out and maintaining his
poster boy good looks.

Carl Williams gave Patty away in marriage to Jack Abbott. Both he and Mary held little hope that the marriage would last.

Paul lent his support to his ex-wife April when she was questioned regarding the death of her husband, Robert Lynch. Christine Blair and John Silva gave legal support.

Paul, Carl and Salena worked on one of their numerous crime cases.

Victor, Nikki and little Victoria spent many happy times at home.

THE NEWMANS

Victor met Nikki when she was a stripper at the Bayou.
He had never seen such a vision of beauty.

Victor Newman is the head of Newman Enterprises, a conglomerate that takes over smaller corporations. His fingers are in so many pies it is difficult to estimate the size of his considerable fortune. All it takes is one look and a snap of his fingers for people to do his bidding. You wouldn't want to have him for an enemy and you would almost be afraid to have him for your friend, although this was not the case with Colonel Douglas Austin. But as intimidating as Victor Newman might be in business matters, he softens when it comes to affairs of the heart.

It's said that many a woman in Genoa City finds him irresistible. When Victor first saw Nikki stripping at the Bayou, he had never before beheld such a vision. Her raw, natural beauty needed nurturing and polishing, and Victor took her home and made her into a refined young woman. They eventually married, and, although their marriage didn't last, they built a relationship that would span a hundred lifetimes. Out of this marriage came two amazing children, Victoria and Nicholas. Victor lavished much love on Victoria and he was Nicholas's best friend.

When Nikki arranged for Victor's mother, Cora Miller, to come to Genoa City, an emotional Victor told his mother that they could never see each other again; that, as far as he was concerned, his mother "died" many years ago, when, as a child, she abandoned him.

After reconciling with Victor, Cora died. Victor realized that love doesn't die and as long as one remembers, they will not be separated.

One Christmas, when Victor and Nikki were not getting along and he was not invited to the ranch for dinner, Victor saw to it that little Nicholas could spend some time with him and place the star atop the Christmas tree.

Victor would do anything to make his two children happy.

Victoria comforted little Nicholas when their mother was taken to the hospital after she fell face down in the snow. She had been drinking and taking pills for her back pain.

Above: Victoria was daddy's little girl, and no matter what, he was there for her.

Right: Victoria toasted Victor on his birthday.

Below: Victor, little Nicholas and Victoria shared the holidays with Douglas and Ashley.

An expectant Hope with Victor and Nikki.

Miguel, the Newmans' faithful manservant, was always overseeing family dinners and celebrations. But more importantly, he was a friend and sounding board to all members of the family. Here he confers with Douglas Austin, Victor's best friend.

Nicholas and Sharon talked with Victor and Nikki.

Whenever Victoria had a problem, she'd bend Ryan's ear. Victor wouldn't approve.

Cole worked on his novel while Victoria looked on. It was Nikki who introduced him to a New York publisher.

Aunt Mamie, her nieces Olivia and Drucilla and Olivia's husband Nathan.

THE HASTINGS AND THE WINTERS

The Hastings and the Winters have brought new blood and stunning dramatic excitement to Genoa City. Both are young professional families determined to meet new challenges with style and class. An agonizing family crisis pitted sisters Drucilla Winters and Olivia Hastings against each other. Lillie Bell asked Olivia, always her favorite, to place her needs above those of Nathan and Nate. Nathan did not feel this was the way to handle the problem, and he gave Olivia an ultimatum: either him and little Nate or her mother. Dru, meanwhile, was torn between her feelings of exclusion—her mother thought Drucilla never did anything right—and her dread at being included in this no-win situation.

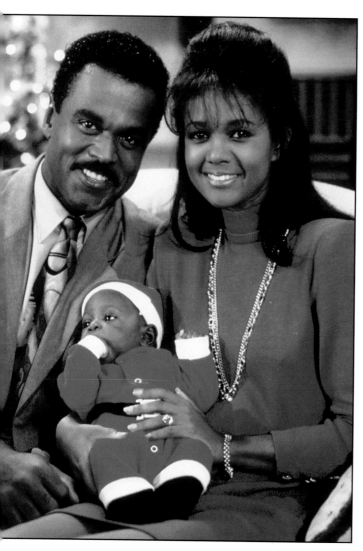

Because of her mother's example, Dru had resolved not to have children. Her husband, Neil, was disturbed by Dru's position, but the couple grew closer when Drucilla did become pregnant and gave birth to their daughter, Lillie. After years of alienation, Neil's brother, Malcolm, came to Genoa City, and they reconciled. What Neil doesn't know, however, is that Malcolm and Dru spent a night together when he was out of town on business. For now, the sisters and the brothers have turned their attention to solving their problems with courage and dignity.

Olivia and Nathan with little Nate observing his very first Christmas.

Neil and Nathan in happier days.

Neil and his brother, Malcolm, are "two of the huggin'-est brothers" actor Shemar Moore (Malcolm) has ever seen!

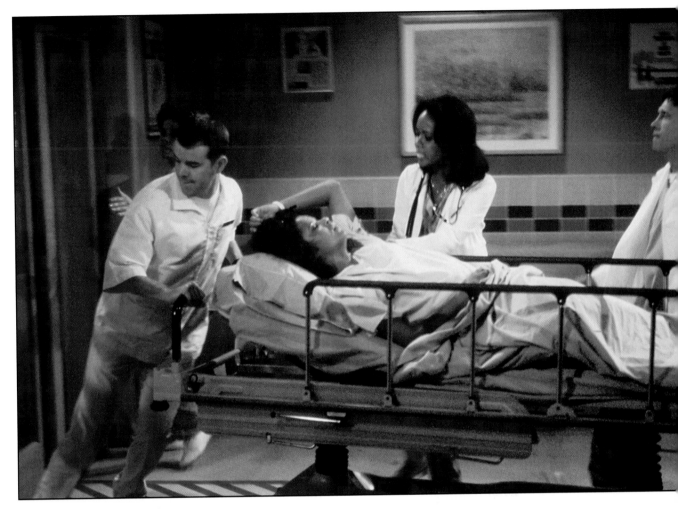

Dru was rushed into the delivery room.

Malcolm offered Neil support as they awaited news of Dru's condition.

Neil and Drucilla welcomed their firstborn, daughter, Lillie.

Olivia presented Drucilla with little Nate's christening gown for Lillie's baptism, the start of a family tradition.

Dru held her baby at the christening ceremony, while Neil and Malcolm looked on.

Aunt Mamie, Neil, Olivia, and Dru exchanged happy talk after the christening.

A portrait of Genoa City's newest family: The Winters.

MOST MEMORABLE MOMENTS OF

Deception and Betrayal

Over the years, "The Young and the Restless" has woven many tangled webs of deception and betrayal. Husbands and wives, brothers and sisters, fathers and sons, friends, foes and lovers all, at some time, either deceive or have been deceived, betray or have been betrayed. Deceivers and betrayers tell lies and keep secrets, build themselves up and tear others down. Motivated by greed, revenge or uncontrollable love, the schemes are sometimes premeditated and painstakingly planned, leaving the "victims" to squirm, and the perpetrators to watch with delight. Sometimes, the deception begins with an innocent mistake and the characters find themselves getting deeper and deeper into the lies with no means of escape. They look for any way out, hoping that their own lives won't be destroyed.

The moment of truth can be shocking or humiliating, infuriating or tragic, explosive or devastating—or all these things rolled into one. The victims are left to pick up the pieces and somehow try to put things back together.

The Dream
That Became a Nightmare

Although Nikki Reed and Greg Foster were so poor that Nikki had to borrow her sister-in-law Chris Brooks's wedding gown to get married in, they looked forward to a happy life together. Greg was just beginning his law practice, and Nikki was, at 16, very young and restless. After some consideration as to what direction her life might take, Nikki decided to pursue a modeling career. That was how she found herself in the offices of the modeling agency headed by Rose DeVille and her partner, Vince Holliday. What Nikki couldn't know was that this agency was a front for a prostitution ring, and the contract stipulated that she owed $1,800 upon signing, work or no work. Her first assignment was to meet a prominent businessman, Mr. Addison, in a hotel across town. Expecting an interview for a modeling gig, Nikki found herself backing away from and pleading with a man who wanted to engage Nikki's services. Addison suddenly collapsed on the floor—dead! A panicked Nikki called Rose and Vince, who rushed to the hotel, cursing out Nikki for the mess she'd gotten them into. They removed the body and dumped it in an alley some distance away. The police caught Tony Baker, a young thug, rifling the victim's pockets and arrested him for felony murder. Greg, of all people, was assigned to the case by the public defender's office. Rose went ballistic when she learned that Tony's lawyer was Nikki's husband, and told Nikki that if she or Vince were implicated in any way, Greg would be a dead man! When the case went to trial, Greg still had no knowledge of Nikki's involvement, but was convinced of Tony's innocence. He was counting on the testimony of a hotel maid who claimed she could identify the blonde who had been with Mr. Addison at the time of his death. Frightened, Nikki wrote Greg a note explaining why she had to leave town. But then Greg's witness said she couldn't make a positive identification after all. When Nikki got word that she was in the clear, she turned her car around, intending to speed home to retrieve the note before Greg would read it. She entered the Exit ramp of the expressway by mistake. It was too late—Nikki crashed into the guardrail and went over the embankment! She hovered between life and death for several days.

Rose and Vince were apprehended for their well-known activities as procurers of young women and they were linked to the case. Conscience-stricken, the maid told Greg in private that the blonde was his wife, and that he could do whatever he wished with that information! Meanwhile, Rose's hitman was on the prowl looking for Greg. For weeks, Greg and Nikki remained in protective custody, sharing a room in a local hotel, barely able to have a conversation. Disillusioned, Greg declared their marriage was over. Nikki sought refuge in the New World communal home, where she felt she would be given unconditional love. Greg despaired over his mother, Liz Foster, who had taken the shot intended for him by the hitman.

Nikki and Greg were certain their marriage would work, for he was her hero and she was his dream girl.

The Centerfold

What made Lauren Fenmore do the things she did? Why did she always spoil the good things in her life, and hurt the people she truly loved? Her mother, JoAnna Manning, said that Lauren was emotionally abused as a child and that her actions were a bid for attention. Maybe. She had certainly played a number of dirty tricks on her adversaries (remember Traci Abbott?) in her teen-age years. So maybe her betrayal and embarrassment of her straight-arrow husband, Paul Williams, were simply the playful, willful, immature and impetuous actions of a young woman who failed to consider the consequences. It all started innocently enough. She took some pictures of Paul in the nude—private shots meant for their eyes alone. But somehow, when the photos were developed, they were sent to Paul at his office, where Amy Lewis was tickled by how much she saw of her boss. An embarrassed Paul showed them to his wife, and then threw them out. But Lauren recovered a few of the negatives, and couldn't resist the temptation to have one made into a poster, which she then presented to Paul. He, of course, blew up, for he thought he had destroyed all of the negatives. But Lauren wasn't to be stopped. She went merrily on her way, and entered one of the pictures into a centerfold contest for the title "Outstanding Professional Male," figuring they could surely use the $10,000 prize. When Lauren told Amy they won, Amy convinced her to refuse the prize money and withdraw her husband from the contest. For Paul would not only be angry, but he had just accepted an appointment to the Mayor's Investigative Commission on Pornography. Lauren tried, but it was too late. The magazines had already hit the streets, and all she could do now was round up her friends to buy up every last issue. Of course that meant every last issue but the few that got away. Paul's mother was shown a copy by one of her churchgoing friends; his father was ribbed unmercifully by his police force friends; and Paul was put in the position of having to resign his appointment to the pornography commission.

It was Paul's shocked Mom who shocked Paul by showing him the centerfold.

All's Fair in Love and War

Tyrone Jackson, a young black law school student from New York City, went undercover in Genoa City to infiltrate the mob and to break Mr. Anthony's syndicate. With the help of his brother, Jazz, and his friend, Private Investigator Andy Richards, Tyrone disguised himself as a white man, and managed to ingratiate himself in Mr. Anthony's eyes by romancing Mr. Anthony's beautiful daughter, Alana. After trying for six months and failing, Tyrone finally convinced Jazz and Andy to help him set up a series of foolproof tactics to make him appear the hero, saving Alana's life. The plan worked and the grateful Mr. Anthony offered Tyrone a job in his "import" company. What Tyrone didn't expect was that he and Alana would fall in love. When Mr. Anthony saw them kissing, he promptly announced their engagement and planned for their wedding to take place within two weeks' time. Tyrone had to act fast. He managed to get the keys to Mr. Anthony's office and gave them to Jazz and Andy.

A Y&R make-up artist transformed Phil Morris from black face to white.

Before the transformation.

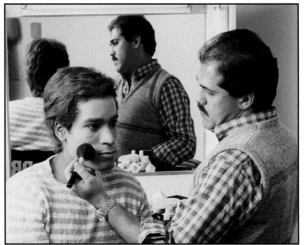

Putting on the finishing touches.

Makeup artist Nick Schillace goes to work.

The files in Mr. Anthony's secret room were the key to cracking the case. An ambush ensued on Tyrone and Alana's wedding day.

Tyrone argued with his brother Jazz over the highly dangerous position in which he'd put himself.

Robert Tyrone posed with his lovely bride, Alana, and his father-in-law, mobster kingpin, Mr. Anthony.

As Mr. Anthony lay on the floor dying, he asked his new son-in-law to take care of his precious daughter, Alana.

As the wedding ceremony was beginning, Jazz and Andy entered a secret room and tripped a remote control alarm system that sealed them behind a concrete door. They lost consciousness for lack of oxygen. Once Tyrone and Alana were pronounced man and wife, Mr. Anthony hastily departed with Tyrone hot on his trail. They both told Alana they would meet her at the reception. Planning on executing Jazz and Andy, Mr. Anthony was instead surprised by the police. A shootout followed, and as Mr. Anthony lay dying, he begged his new son-in-law to take care of his precious Alana. Later that evening, Tyrone was faced with the awesome burden of compounding his wife's grief by disclosing his true identity. With his back to her, Tyrone began to spread cold cream over his face.

Tyrone was about to reveal to Alana the man she really married.

Alana was devastated that Tyrone thought she couldn't love him just because he was black.

TYRONE: (WITHOUT TURNING)
> *Alana, I'm sorry...truly sorry. But I've already told you...this can't wait any longer. I...think you'll understand why as soon as I turn around.*

ALANA: (UTTERLY MYSTIFIED, TEARS IN HER EYES)
> *Then turn around...*

TYRONE: (SOFTLY)
> *Forgive me...*
> (HE REACHES UP, TAKES OFF HIS WIG...
> AND AS HE DOES, HE TURNS SLOWLY.)

ALANA: (UTTERLY TERRIFIED AND DISORIENTED)
> *Who—Who are you? What's happening?*

TYRONE: (GENTLY)
> *Alana, it's me...*

ALANA: (BECOMING A BIT HYSTERICAL)
> *No, no! No, you're not my husband!! You're not the man I married! Dear God, what happened to Robert?! What have you done with him?!!*

TYRONE: *Alana...I was Robert. But my real name's Tyrone.*

ALANA: (HYSTERICAL)
> *I know...Robert Tyrone...*

TYRONE: *No. Tyrone Jackson. I'm Jazz Jackson's brother. It was all makeup. A cover.*

His Brother's Wife

Ashley Abbott and photographer Blade didn't have a picture-perfect marriage. At almost every turn, Ashley felt that Blade was hiding something from her. She knew he'd changed his name from Alex Bladeson in an effort to escape an unhappy past and the memory of his late, evil twin brother, Rick. She also knew he'd lied to her about his past relationship with Mari Jo Mason, the woman with whom Ashley's own brother, Jack, was now involved. Blade denied Ashley's accusations of clandestine meetings with Mari Jo, even though Ashley had seen them together with her own two eyes! What neither of them realized was that Rick, Blade's twin, was very much alive and in Genoa City, poised to wreak havoc on their lives.

In an effort to get their relationship back on track, Ashley and Blade took a romantic vacation to St. Thomas. When they returned, Blade's newfound talents in the bedroom greatly impressed Ashley. What she didn't know was that Rick had also flown to St. Thomas, knocked out his brother, locked him up and assumed his identity. So her "husband" was really her husband's brother!

John learned Blade was a man of principle—a quality he admired and respected.

Ashley and Blade married and planned a happy life together, until his brother, Rick, implemented his devious plan.

Mari Jo Mason had a relationship with Rick Bladeson before she came to Genoa City. She hoped to keep their past a secret.

Rick read up on Ashley so that he could assume his brother's identity and play the role of her husband.

When Ashley confided in Mari Jo about her improved love life, Mari Jo figured out Rick's diabolical deception but never said anything to Ashley. Rick may have stumbled a few times in his scheming—he didn't recognize Ashley's sister, Traci, at a family celebration, and he wasn't an expert photographer like his brother. But he pulled it off, and in the process fell in love with Ashley.

When Blade finally managed to escape and returned to Genoa City, he was enraged at his brother for sleeping with his wife, and he told Rick to leave or risk going to jail for fraud. Rick said he'd leave, but didn't. Fearing for Blade's safety, Mari Jo begged him to meet at her office—she had to warn him about Rick's threats. Rick and Ashley were together when the phone rang. It was Blade checking up on Ashley. When he heard his brother's voice, he raced home. Rick told Ashley he had to tend to an emergency at the studio, but he wouldn't be long. Rick waited outside the Abbott estate to confront his brother. Instead, the police arrived with the news that Blade had been killed in a train wreck on his way home. How could that be? Ashley thought. He'd just left to go to the studio. In one sickening, horrific moment of denouement, the truth came crashing down on Ashley. Rick confessed to changing places with his brother on numerous occasions. He professed his love to her, but so repulsed and humiliated was Ashley that she quickly jetted off to Paris to try to rebuild her life, alone.

Ashley had trouble accepting Blade's lies, and considered filing for divorce. They were both unaware his twin brother, Rick, was at the root of the problem.

Ashley and "Blade's" love life greatly improved when his brother, Rick, took his place.

Prominent Genoa City Photographer Killed in Car-Train Collision

Many persons feel at this stage that some legal action is forthcoming but it now becomes common knowledge that there is pressure from the inside which will materially change the aspect of the case.

An immediate investigation is assured and indications are that some new light will be shed on the situation in the near future. Available facts seem vague but authorities feel that time will disclose some means of arriving at a solution.

Future plans will, of necessity, have great bearing on the situation as it now stands. Decisions will have to be made of the actual planning of the project will take considerable time but it is felt that these steps are very important.

Many persons feel at this that some legal action is

ALEX "BLADE" BLADESON

Future plans will, of nec have great bear

Dungeons and Dragons

Victor Newman was riding high in 1980! He was not only testing his mettle as head of Chancellor Industries, but he had also acquired several other new challenges—a photography studio and a new bride, Julia, a Jabot model, from whom he was keeping a momentous secret. Victor had had a vasectomy; babies were simply not a part of his plan! He encouraged Julia to become friendly with Michael Scott, the photographer who ran his studio, reasoning that if she posed for him, Victor would be able to judge the caliber of his work. But Victor didn't bargain for the exposure of another secret. His former private secretary, Eve Howard, disclosed to Julia that Victor had fathered her child, Cole Howard, one night long ago. Eve was now seeking child support from Victor. This disclosure shook Julia, and sent her straight into the arms of Michael Scott. It wasn't long before Julia informed Victor that he was about to become a father. At first he thought his doctor had botched the vasectomy, but tests proved that it was 100% effective—unless, of course, Victor had made love too soon after the operation. Victor tormented Julia, asking if she would choose him over her baby. He said he considered a baby to be an intrusion upon their lives. Julia was devastated, and Victor convinced her that a few days at the hospital would do her a world of good. Victor then had Julia's hospital room bugged, and found out that Michael and Julia were planning to meet in Vancouver and head together to Geneva. Springing into action, Victor hired a contractor to build a bomb shelter in the basement of his ranch, complete with the latest electronic video and audio equipment. He then lured Michael to the ranch and locked him in the shelter. When Julia came home, Victor tormented Michael by having him watch their lovemaking on the TV mon-

Newlyweds Victor and Julia Newman were newcomers to Genoa City.

itor. Julia, meanwhile, wondered why Michael hadn't contacted her from Vancouver, until she received a Victor-engineered "Dear Jane" cable. It was an accident when Julia came upon one of the hidden TV monitors, which revealed the imprisoned Michael! The two eventually figured out the secret code that would open the door to the dungeon. Victor and Michael scuffled on the stairs, knocking down Julia, who was rushed to the hospital and miscarried. The baby proved to be Victor's, after all. Soon, Julia and Michael left the country, with Victor kissing Julia good-bye, saying he would never see her again.

Julia Newman was greatly troubled about a number of things she had found out about Victor, and Michael Scott offered sympathetic advice.

Victor and Michael discuss business.

A record of Victor's vasectomy.

Victor had an elaborate system of TV monitors and audio equipment installed so that he could monitor Michael Scott's every move. He also made Michael witness his and Julia's lovemaking.

Creating the Bomb Shelter

To create the effect of cement being poured for Victor's dungeon, the special effects department spent three days cooking 55 gallon tubs of oatmeal over butane torch heater units. Onstage, a forklift and ramp were used to hoist the tubs and pour the oatmeal down the cement chute into concrete forms. After the "contractors" smoothed the "cement," the camera would stop rolling so that the oatmeal could be shoveled back into the tubs and forklifted to the top again to create a continuous flow of "concrete." According to Y&R production designer Bill Hultstrom, the stage became a "glutinous mass of tracked-around oatmeal!"

John Abbott and his son, Jack, were close. What could possibly happen to alienate them?

A Puzzling Affair

What was Jill to do? Mamie was blaming her for causing Traci's automobile accident (as if she was the one who was driving! Hell, she wasn't even in the car!) and Dina was ratting on her to John about being pregnant or something (she wasn't; she just said she was!)! A word here, a word there, and in no time at all, things got out of hand, and John and Jill were in the middle of a raging argument! Jill rushed out of the house. She wasn't going to stay there, blizzard or no blizzard! She drove blindly through the swirling snow right into a ditch! The only person she could reach was her stepson, Jack. He had her on the car phone…then static! Jack jumped into his Jeep and went looking for her. When he found her, they just happened to discover this perfect little summer home…a port in a storm! In no time at all, boy scout Jack had a raging fire going, and he was comforting Jill, stroking her hair, gently kissing away the tears. Well, you know, one thing led to another, and pretty soon they were rolling all over the floor and making passionate love on this nice bearskin rug. And would you believe that someone was recording all these Kodak moments? Jack and Jill discovered this later when they each received mysterious gray envelopes at the office and the Abbott home. Lindsey, an early, discarded girlfriend of Jack's whom he didn't even remember, admitted to being the shutterbug. All she wanted from Jack was a big boost up the corporate ladder at Jabot! But when it seemed Jack wasn't taking her seriously—or at least wasn't acting quickly enough—she decided to let everyone know about Jack's betrayal. So she sold the negatives to Katherine Chancellor, who saw a way to get even with Jill. She made the photos into a puzzle and sent them piece by piece...to John. But of course, she wouldn't want to totally destroy her dear friend by revealing that the man in the puzzle was his son, Jack, so Katherine doctored up the puzzle. Nevertheless, despite her best efforts, the truth did come out. When John later discovered that he had been cuckolded by his own son, he suffered a stroke that sent him to the hospital. When he recovered, he kicked both Jill and Jack out, refusing to have anything to do with either one of them.

Maybe Jack could smooth things over for John...patch up the argument he'd had with Jill...

If Jack played up to Lindsey, he could get those negatives away from her!

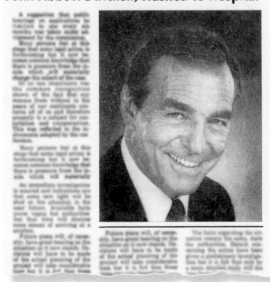

When John pieced the puzzle together, he would learn of Jack's betrayal.

John Abbott Stricken, Rushed to Hospital

Nikki had come to tell Victor she was well. She suddenly felt very sick.

A Kiss to Die For

It was the kiss that launched a thousand lies. Nikki had rushed all the way home from the hospital to tell Victor she was in remission, only to find her husband kissing Ashley Abbott in a remote corner of the ranch! They were hugging, sharing tender intimacies! How dare he? Nikki'd show him! First she had to warn her sister, Casey, not to tell him about her apparent recovery.

Ashley was so concerned over the feelings of others, how could Victor not love her?

She had really been sick, but now she was well pretending to be sick! When Victor suggested they call in a specialist, Nikki knew the ruse would be up. She painstakingly made a "farewell" videotape that she instructed be played after her death, and left it in plain sight for Victor to find, which he did. He cried his eyes out. He was so emotional that he told his archrival, Jack Abbott, Nikki was dying.

Nikki was having such fun. She had to look really sick, so she applied some blue makeup to give her a ghastly complexion. *My God,* Victor thought, *her illness is progressing more quickly than I thought it would!* Nikki next pleaded for some time alone with Jack. How could Victor refuse? He generously gave them some privacy. Nikki wanted to go on a picnic, and for once, Jack didn't know how to act—being on a picnic with a dying woman! Nikki begged Jack to make her feel like a woman, one last time. Nikki couldn't contain herself any longer, and she told Jack the truth. Half loving it, half fearful of what Victor would say to her when he found out, Jack reminded Nikki that she was playing a dangerous game. But, what the hell, he'd be her coconspirator. Together, they set up an appointment to have a mortician come to the ranch to make her funeral arrangements. Victor was so moved that he suggested they take that cruise Nikki always wanted but for which he could never make time. Nikki appreciated the thought, but said she'd rather spend her remaining days at the ranch. Next she thought she'd go on a shopping spree—fur coats, expensive pearls, the works! What fun! Then Jack came up with a swell idea: bleed Victor for a large chunk of Mergeron America stock, so Nikki would have the pleasure of giving it to little Victoria while she was still living, in trust, of course, but with the interest paying off to Nikki. After all, she'd be needing it to live on when Victor found out. And she played the game to the hilt.

Victor had caught on, but he had to pretend he didn't, because, if he divorced Nikki as he wanted to, then she would get half of his estate! But poor, vulnerable cry-her-eyes-out Nikki couldn't go on with this any longer. She told Victor the truth. It was all because of that kiss she saw him give Ashley.

The ramifications of Nathan's affair with Keesha would be far more explosive than anyone expected.

Broken Vows, Shattered Lives

Nathan Hastings betrayed his wife, Olivia, and in the process put their lives and the life of their son in jeopardy. Feeling neglected by Olivia's preoccupation with her work, Nathan took up with Keesha Monroe. Lipstick on his collar and his lack of interest in his love life at home raised Olivia's suspicions. She asked Nathan's boss, Private Investigator Paul Williams, to find out whether Nathan might be having an affair. Paul managed to get a confession out of Nathan, but Nathan lied and said it was over. Meanwhile, he told Keesha to lay low for a while because Olivia was asking too many questions. Nathan and Olivia mended fences, and his renewed interest eased her mind. But Nathan was still drawn to Keesha, and they resumed their torrid affair. When she gave him an ultimatum: "Leave Olivia or lose me," Nathan couldn't commit. But before they broke it off, Neil spied Nathan and Keesha together and told Dru.

Upset over Nathan, Keesha started to date good guy Malcolm, who couldn't wait for his family to meet his new lady. Olivia thought it was a coincidence that Malcolm was dating a new patient of hers (Keesha had gone to check out Nathan's wife on the pretext of needing a physical). Dru was incensed Nathan could hurt her sister this way, and warned Keesha to stay

Nathan and Olivia were happily married—or so she thought.

Nathan would often call Keesha from the office, hoping to hide his affair from his wife.

Keesha was in love with Nathan and longed for his physical presence in her life. She issued him an ultimatum: her or Olivia.

away from Nathan. Malcolm and Olivia were still in the dark. Poor Malcolm couldn't figure out why his family disliked Keesha, the woman he was falling in love with. Olivia confided in Dru that she hoped to be pregnant by Christmastime.

Keesha then began receiving telephone calls from her old boyfriend, Stan, but she refused to talk to him. She confessed to Neil that she was in love with Malcolm, and begged him not to tell his brother about her affair with Nathan—she'd now officially ended it. Keesha soon realized if she wanted a future with Malcolm, she should be straight with him. She confessed the affair to him, and Malcolm was crushed. Keesha then looked to Stan for a shoulder to cry on, only to find out he'd died of complications from AIDS. And he was probably infected when

Dru found out about Nathan's affair with Keesha. She threatened to turn him in, but was afraid of the pain it would cause her sister, Olivia.

When Olivia's family found out about her husband's affair, they rallied their support around her.

they were seeing each other! Horrified, Keesha went for an AIDS test, purposely seeing a doctor other than Olivia. But when the test results came back positive, Olivia, as her primary physician, was the one who broke the news to her. "You must inform all of your sexual partners," Olivia urged her patient.

Olivia's world turned upside down when Dru finally told her Nathan and Keesha had an affair. If that wasn't enough, Nathan informed Olivia that he and their son, Nate, both recently suffered cuts in a playground accident! The confrontation between Olivia and Nathan was explosive. How could he destroy their marriage like this? How could he carry on with another woman and still make love to her? And how could he possibly be so stupid as to have unprotected sex with this other woman?! Did he realize now that because of his betrayal, they were all in danger of contracting HIV? She ordered Nathan out of her life and vowed to do anything…anything, to keep him away from her son.

Little Nate couldn't understand why his Daddy wasn't around. He just wanted them to be together. The pictures he drew brought tears to Olivia's eyes.

Genoa City Chronicle

Industrialist Victor Newman Dies In Fiery Car Crash

Resurrection

The residents of Genoa City thought Victor Newman died a fiery death. He had left town, destination unknown, when he concluded that the three most important women in his life—Nikki, Victoria and Ashley—were all fed up with his manipulative ways. While on his journey, he was attacked at knifepoint. The thief stole his money, his belongings and his Rolls Royce, and left Victor on a deserted road. He wound up on a Kansas farm and made friends with the owner, Hope Adams. Meanwhile, back in Genoa City, the authorities informed Victor's family that they had found his car at the bottom of a ravine; it had apparently careened off the highway and exploded. Victor's remains were charred beyond recognition, but his ID bracelet and a piece of his driver's license led the police to declare that it was Victor who died in the accident. Victor's realization—via Douglas, whom he had contacted—that his loved ones were getting on with their lives—without him—was enough to convince Victor that it was time for him to start over as well. In Kansas—with Hope. But when Victor heard a news report that Jack Abbott had taken over Newman Enterprises, he set a plan in motion to reclaim what was his. Victor anonymously sent out invitations to a gathering at the Colonnade Room. In a delicious moment of shock and surprise, Victor's guests saw that Victor was very much alive! He left quickly to reunite with his children, and later took great pleasure in spinning around in his desk chair, revealing himself to his awestruck rival, Jack Abbott!

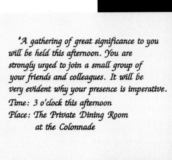

"A gathering of great significance to you will be held this afternoon. You are strongly urged to join a small group of your friends and colleagues. It will be very evident why your presence is imperative.
Time: 3 o'clock this afternoon
Place: The Private Dining Room at the Colonnade

Victor Newman's family and friends grieve at his memorial service.

Genoa City residents were invited to a mysterious gathering, never suspecting Victor was the host! Douglas greeted
the guests, who wondered why they were summoned.

Victor Newman was about to rock Genoa City with his return from the dead!

Upon his return, Victor shared a tender moment with his children.

John and Jill were thunder- struck by Victor's return. John saw it as another serious setback for the Abbott family business.

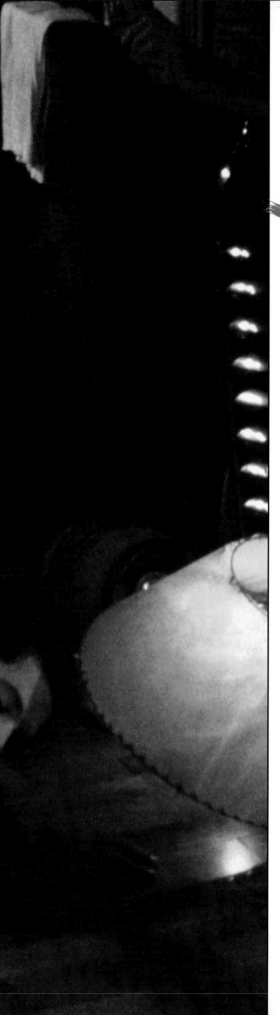

Crimes of Passion ...and More

Crimes of passion are the essence of drama. Storytellers not only weave tangled webs of intertwined and ruined lives, but they attempt to explain the forces and circumstances that lead people to commit the ultimate act. Few do this better than the creative team of master storytellers at "The Young and the Restless." Yet, as heinous as some of these crimes might be, the writers never lose sight of their responsibility to their audience. In more cases than not, the psychological fallout of the crime on the victim, the victim's family and friends, the perpetrator and the perpetrator's family and friends are presented in provocative fashion. So entangled and Byzantine are these webs, that viewers become engrossed in the twists and turns of the story, leaving them much room for thought and reflection.

Vanessa's Moment of Vengeance

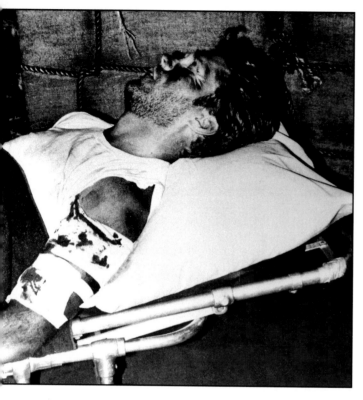

Who would've thought that another fire involving Lucas Prentiss would send him home for a reunion with his family?

To never forget the disastrous fire that disfigured her and tore her family apart, Vanessa chose to wear a veil that covered the lower part of her face rather than to undergo plastic surgery. She saved the life of her beloved son, Lance, and her younger son, Lucas—who had accidentally started the fire. Lucas left Genoa City to roam the high seas, but did return home a number of years later, ironically after becoming a hero by saving people in another fire in Hong Kong.

Lance eventually married Lorie Brooks, the high-spirited daughter of Genoa City's prominent newspaperman, Stuart Brooks. Vanessa would have much preferred that her oldest son marry Lorie's sister, Leslie, whom she felt was better suited for Lance, so she did everything she could to wreck that marriage. She even managed to create a situation that sent Lance straight into Leslie's arms, and he unknowingly fathered a son. But he returned to Lorie, while Lucas married Leslie and raised Lance's son, Brooks, as if he were his own.

Some years later, Lance divorced Lorie and Lucas fell in love with her. Then, Leslie divorced Lucas. Lorie and Lucas were now raising Brooks. Somehow Lorie and Lance found their way back to each other. On the eve of their remarriage, Vanessa knew she had to do something drastic to prevent it from happening. This time she would concoct the most perfect scheme—one that could not fail. For Vanessa had recently learned that she was terminally ill, and she had nothing to lose by putting a diabolical plan into action.

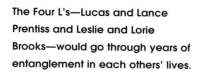

The Four L's—Lucas and Lance Prentiss and Leslie and Lorie Brooks—would go through years of entanglement in each others' lives.

Lance and Lorie couldn't get each other out of their systems. Their love affair was tempestuous. Here they spend a quiet moment contemplating the future.

Offering to baby-sit her grandson, Brooks, Vanessa typed a chilling letter on Lorie's personalized stationery incriminating Lorie, and she mailed it to herself. When the letter arrived, Vanessa put it in a place where Lance would be sure to find it. Then Vanessa put on her best face and gave Lance and Lorie her blessing, telling them she was now at peace with their decision to remarry.

After a few days, Vanessa phoned Lorie, insisting she be allowed to come for a visit accompanied by her son, Lucas. Surprised but anxious to make peace with Vanessa before the wedding, Lorie agreed. Leaving the two women alone, Lucas went upstairs to Brooks's room to spend some time with him. Vanessa then told Lorie she'd like to go outside on the balcony as it was such a nice day. Trusting that they were on the right track at last, Lorie was nothing short of amenable. The moment was at hand.

Lucas blamed himself for his mother's disfigurement, but mother and son were able to put this part of their past behind them.

Although Lucas married Leslie to give Leslie and Lance's son, Brooks, his name, he was always attracted to Lorie.

LORIE: *I wonder, Vanessa, if you have any idea how happy you've made me today. It's something I never thought would happen. You and I—that we could be friends. It's the most fantastic wedding gift you could ever give me. You said you wanted to talk about the wedding...Vanessa?*

(A MOMENT'S PAUSE, THEN VANESSA TURNS, FACES LORIE, AND BEGINS SHOUTING SO THAT NEIGHBORS WILL OVERHEAR.)

VANESSA: *I don't care what you want, Lorie!! I have a duty to my son and to Brooks! You have no right to impose your selfishness on their lives! I will not permit them to live a lie any longer just because that's what you want for yourself!*

LORIE: *Vanessa, what—?*

VANESSA: *Don't tell me you know best! You have no right to say that! Don't you dare threaten me! Stop it, Lorie! Let go of me! You won't get away with this! What do you think you're doing?! Let go of me! Have you gone mad! Lorie—for God's sake— I'm going to fall! Don't! Please! Help me! Help me, please! Don't do this to me!*

After Vanessa's death, Lance comforted Lorie, while Lucas wondered how such a terrible "accident" could have happened.

(LORIE IS STUNNED, TERRIFIED AS VANESSA DISAPPEARS OVER THE BALCONY, AND AS WE HEAR VANESSA'S EERIE SCREAM, SHE DESCENDS TO THE EARTH BELOW.)

Repercussions

Volunteer Chris Foster met Nancy Becker at the Legal Aid Clinic. Nancy was seeking advice for her husband, Ron, who was being held in jail on charges of possible rape and burglary. She insisted he was railroaded by a woman he had met at a bar who then invited him to her apartment and yelled "Rape!" The woman's neighbors detained Ron until the police came, and he was forced to cop a plea—burglary instead of rape. Chris didn't believe this story at all and, remembering her own assault by a sadistic monster, she felt instant revulsion for Ron. But her heart went out to the delicate, shy Nancy and her small child, Karen. With Ron in jail, his family was suffering; Nancy had diabetes, and Karen needed the love and attention of parents who were able to take care of her.

Ron was released after the charges were dismissed because of insufficient evidence. But it didn't take him long to get in trouble again, this time for assaulting Peggy Brooks, Chris's sister! At Chris's insistence, Peggy brought charges against Ron, and he was arrested again. When the case went to trial, Peggy had to relive the entire devastating experience. The jury believed him to be guilty, but Ron was released once again for lack of concrete evidence, and he left town. Many people, though, were affected by the fallout from his crimes; Peggy, for one, had to constantly repress feelings of insecurity and felt she could never trust a man again; Nancy had a mental breakdown and required institutionalization; and Chris and Snapper took little Karen into their home. Chris grew so attached to Karen that Snapper feared she would be crushed if the child was taken away.

Then Ron returned to Genoa City a changed man. He promised Snapper and Chris he wouldn't give them any more trouble, and relinquished all claims to Karen. Buoyed by his resolve, Chris blissfully started adoption proceedings, only to have Ron break his promise. Miraculously, a recovering Nancy wanted her daughter back. It broke Chris's heart when Karen called Nancy "Mommy," and she realized that Karen belonged with her mother. The Becker family left Genoa City for good, and a heartbroken Chris left Snapper to search for her own identity.

Ron Becker claimed he loved his little daughter, Karen, but he knew that Chris and Snapper Foster would be able to give her a better home.

Ron never thought his catatonic wife would recover. He also never faulted himself for her institutionalization.

Misplaced Love

For Patty Williams, marrying Jack Abbott was a dream come true. For Jack, marrying Patty meant assuming the presidency of Jabot—his father's wedding present to him.

Patty Abbott suddenly turned the small handgun she was pointing at her own head on her husband Jack after he suggested in desperation that she shoot him instead. She did, three times, and then blocked the entire scene from her memory. What drove the docile Patty over the edge? Jack's unbearable psychological abuse, his boozing and scandalous womanizing had caused Patty to miscarry. Now, on the eve of their first wedding anniversary, when she once again broached the subject of having another child, Patty overheard her husband confiding to Jill that he didn't want a family. After all, didn't he marry Patty because it was the only way for him to become president of Jabot?

Patty's father, police detective Carl Williams, assigned himself to the case, pledging to track down the person who shot his irascible son-in-law. But why wasn't Jack talking? Who was he protecting? And why was Patty now "terrorizing" Jack by not only pretending to have no knowledge about what she did, but also by her solicitous concern for his recovery? When Carl Williams learned that Jack had been protecting his own precious little girl, he couldn't have been more mortified or apologetic. Patty's psychiatrist came up with the perfect way for Patty to recall what she had done: set up a similar stress situation under controlled conditions—only this time put a gun loaded with blanks in Patty's purse. But Patty left her purse behind and bought a handgun on the way home. In the reenactment, Patty was able to recall the terrible crime she committed, but stopped short of duplicating the act. Jack plea-bargained on her behalf with the district attorney and placed the blame squarely on himself. When the repentant Jack suggested to Patty that they try again to make their marriage work, he was totally unprepared for her strong resolve to put an end to their loveless union.

Mary Williams prayed with her daughter, Patty, for Jack's recovery in the hospital chapel.

After Jack's shooting, John Abbott comforted his daughter Traci while his concerned oldest daughter Ashley looked on.

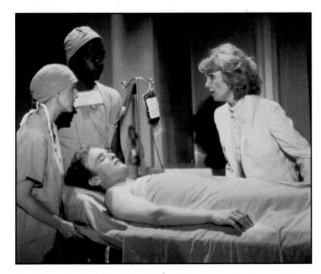

Jack's estranged mother, Dina Mergeron, hastened to her son's bedside.

Ashley greeted Jack's close friend Gina Roma at the hospital.

Jeanne Cooper welcomed the opportunity to play a dual role just as long as she wouldn't be playing twins.

The Doppelganger, Katherine and Miss Boo Hoo

Sometimes one and one equals one because two would be far too much. This might well describe the dual roles of Katherine Sterling and Marge that Jeanne Cooper was asked to play. Clint Radisson, Rex Sterling's ex-cell mate in his less savory days, was literally licking his chops over the great idea he had concocted. For Clint did a double take when he came upon gum-chewing, lip-smacking, tough-talking Marge, a waitress in a diner on the edge of town. Swift at recognizing the elements that go into devising a world-class scam, Clint couldn't believe his eyes: he was looking at a dead ringer for Katherine Sterling!

True, Marge's red hair would have to be dyed blond, and her gold tooth would have to be replaced with a porcelain one. The cigarette she wore behind her ear would have to go, as would her beer drinking. She would have to mimic everything about Katherine precisely—mannerisms, diction, penmanship, walking, dressing, undressing, having sex with Rex (gut instinct, follow his lead—whatever worked), even down to the removal of her appendix because Katherine had just had hers removed (and the scars had to be identical!). Once a test run in a restaurant assured Clint that Marge could pull the ruse off without a hitch, the substitution would be made and Katherine whisked away to an out-of-the-way cabin where she would be held prisoner until her estate, Chancellor Industries and all of her holdings were unloaded, without Rex suspecting a thing! Marge, of course, would become Katherine Sterling, the lady of the manor.

What they didn't plan for was that the very pregnant Esther, Katherine's loyal maid, whom captors Morey and Lil dubbed "Miss Boo Hoo," had come along for the ride. The scheme almost went off, except that Katherine's son Brock happened upon Esther in the hospital when her pregnancy got out of hand, and Esther whispered in his ear that Marge was not the real Katherine, his mother. It didn't take Brock long to get Marge to confess and to enlist her aid in freeing the two ladies.

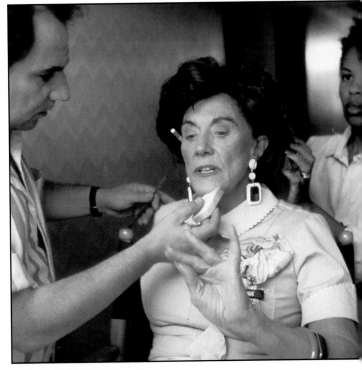

Jeanne Cooper's transformation to Marge.

When Clint spotted Marge at the diner, he did a double take. Was Marge sure she didn't have a sister named Katherine Sterling?

Marge and the Sterlings' new servants frantically tried to get rid of the odor of smoke after their card game!

While Esther stewed over their predicament, Katherine tried to figure a way out.

"Will the real Katherine Sterling step forward?" asked Morey.

Beating a Rap

Danny Romalotti wowed the crowd in Genoa City, but he had to face the music when he was confronted by police and arrested. The charge: dealing drugs. Unbeknownst to Danny, David Kimble had planted cocaine in Danny's dressing room, and then anonymously called the cops to turn him in. Danny thought he was free and clear when the lab report showed no trace of drugs in his system. But the prosecution had enough evidence to bring the case before the grand jury, and Danny was forced to cancel his concert dates and postpone his marriage to Cricket, who stood by him. She even hoped Danny would say yes to an impromptu wedding. But he couldn't marry her, not when his future looked so bleak. Then the court was ordered to turn the informant's tape over to Danny's lawyer, John Silva. They knew they could identify a disguised voice—David had used an accent when he called—but they needed to have a recording of the person's "real" voice. David started to sweat. He'd left a message on Danny's machine and realized he had better get rid of the tape. Done! Then the coke dealer who went to jail threatened to expose David's involvement unless David came up with a very large sum of money to keep him quiet.

A disguised David Kimble planted cocaine in Danny's dressing room.

Danny's career, and the life he planned with Cricket, were threatened when he was falsely accused of selling cocaine.

Without a search warrant and because they had an anonymous tip, the prosecution's case wasn't as airtight as they thought it was, so the charges were dropped. The *National Inquisitor*'s front-page story saying Danny beat the charges on a technicality raised his ire. He was determined to prove his innocence. But how? Cricket remembered that Danny had flowers delivered to his dressing room the night of the concert, which meant someone else had access and the drugs could have been planted! The case was reopened, but it wasn't without risk; if convicted, Danny faced six years in prison. The jury viewed a videotape showing a guard delivering flowers and determined he was in the room long enough to plant the evidence. The final blow to the prosecution came when the guard's uniform was discovered stashed in an air-conditioning vent. The verdict came back: not guilty! Danny's name was finally cleared and he immediately whisked Cricket away to Hawaii, where they were married!

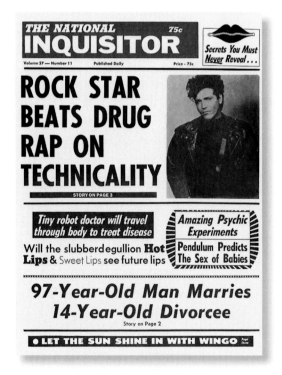

The "rags" reported that Danny was cleared on a technicality. The truth was that he'd been framed.

Danny ordered the case reopened to rightfully clear his name.

Woman on the Edge

Robert Lynch lay mortally wounded. He had pushed his wife too far.

Paul Williams was content to let the past remain in the past. His mother, chronic meddler Mary Williams, pushed him into contacting his ex-wife April to inquire about their daughter, Heather. But that was about as far as Paul wanted to go. After all, April did say that she was very happy in her second marriage to dentist husband Robert Lynch and that Heather was a well-adjusted young lady doing well in her studies in an upscale boarding school. Why intrude upon this picture of apparent harmony and serenity, and upset Heather by introducing her to an "absentee" father she never knew existed?

Then why did it nag at him? Why was Paul compelled to phone April again, and then jet to New York because he didn't like the nervous edge in her voice, which made him think she was covering something up? When Paul got there, she was badly bruised and admitted that her husband had been physically abusive. She agreed to return to Genoa City with Paul and spend some time with her ex-mother-in-law, Mary. She left Robert a note saying she'd gone to visit her mother. Mary talked April into joining a spousal abuse support group in Genoa City, but she felt she was different from all the other women, both in her comfortable lifestyle and in having a husband who cared about her and who adored Heather. Didn't he always bring her flowers after he smacked her around a little, and wasn't it partly her fault for aggravating him? Maybe if she

April read a report on domestic violence.

April's mug shot.

in New York; neighbors were un-aware that the couple was having problems; Heather said that, as far as she knew, her parents got along peacefully; and April did have a gun on her person when she went to see Robert! Things did not look good as the trial progressed, even though Mary, Paul and her friends from the shelter testified on April's behalf. In the end it was April's own riveting tes-timony and a doctor's report detailing injuries resulting from spousal abuse—not, as alleged, from an auto-mobile accident—that won her a sus-pended sentence.

tried to be a better wife…? Robert Lynch, meanwhile, fol-lowed April to Genoa City, and got her to spend a few nights with him in his hotel. She decided to attend one last group therapy session, and one of her friends, suspecting she'd be returning to New York with Robert, gave her a gun for protection. April returned to the hotel to see her husband, and they got into a violent argument in which he threatened the welfare of her daughter. In one awesome moment, she picked up a letter opener from the desk, plunging it into his back and killing him. When April was arrested for Robert's murder, the investigation resulted in several allegations and brought many new alleged facts to light: Paul and April were having an affair; there were no reports of Robert's abusive behavior on the police blotter

Genoa City Chronicle — Page 3

Lynch Indicted for Murder

APRIL LYNCH

John Silva cross-examined Paul Williams, April's ex-husband.

April, Christine Blair and John Silva
reacted to damaging testimony.

Esther Valentine proudly showed off her house servants: butler Rex Sterling and maid Katherine Sterling.

Esther and the Knight in Tarnished Armor

Taking off that silly little maid's apron and cap Katherine Sterling required her to wear always constituted a moment in Esther Valentine's life. Little did Esther know that in the days ahead she'd be experiencing many really big moments, ranging from unbelievable happiness to shock-

ing discovery, and finally, profound grief. It all began when Esther answered an ad in the *Chronicle*'s personals column that was placed by a man named Norman Peterson. An investment banker, he was coming to Genoa City just to see her! Esther fluttered—she didn't know where to begin, what to think, what to say, what to do. This gorgeous mansion…would it be possible? Would the Sterlings allow her to pass herself off as the lady of the manor? Just for a day? What harm would there be in a little charade? At first her employers balked, and said it was unthinkable and unethical and that it was no way to begin a relationship! But there they were bowing—Rex in his stiff tux and Katherine in Esther's own silly little apron and cap—with their forced little smiles, waiting on Esther and her handsome gentleman caller. Katherine, of course, could have wrung Esther's silly little neck for constantly ringing for them to come to the table. As for Norman, there was something about him Katherine just didn't like. Moreover, she didn't trust him, and playing maidservant to the likes of him just once was too much. So she made Esther fess up, but Norman insisted he had something to tell her first. He was a barber, not an investment banker. When Esther had her turn at the confessional, though, Norman wanted to dump her, until she let it slip that she was in Mrs. Sterling's will.

"Let's get married," Norman said. Esther could hardly keep her feet on the ground. Mrs. Sterling said they could have the ceremony in the mansion, and that she'd take care of everything. She hired an actor to play the role of the minister, and the ceremony went off without a hitch. Norman wasted no time. When the couple returned from their honeymoon, he wanted to start a family right away. Then he had the new Mrs. Peterson ask Katherine for her inheritance so they could invest in their children's future. Katherine said sure, but only if the money was deposited in Esther's name only. This was too much for Norman, and he asked for a divorce, telling Esther that he was going to seek half the inheritance as his share of the divorce settlement. Katherine then told him the jig was up; that he wasn't legally married to Esther, and he'd better disappear. Esther, of course, went to pieces. Norman sneaked back into the house armed with a gun, and began to rifle through the safe. Rex caught him in the act and, in a stunning moment, Norman shot him dead, escaping before either Katherine or Esther could stop him. That night, poor Esther learned that her knight wore tarnished armor, and a man whom she loved and respected so much had to pay with his life for her own foolishness.

Katherine gave stage directions to the actor/minister she hired to officiate at Esther and Norman's wedding.

Esther and Norman had no way of knowing that their wedding was playacting, while Katherine played director in the background.

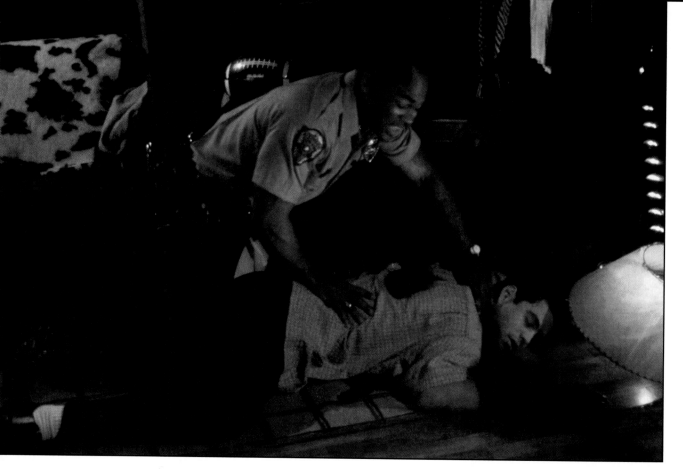

Poor Little Rich Boy

When the cops arrived on the scene, they found Matt had been shot, and Nicholas was holding the weapon.

Nicholas Newman had the world by the tail. He had terrific parents; his sister, Victoria, was his "best bud"; and to top it all off, he'd proposed marriage to the girl of his dreams, Sharon Collins. But Nicholas's nemesis, Matt Clark, wasn't about to sit idly by and let Nicholas be happy. Nick, after all, was the reason Sharon jilted him, and Matt wanted revenge. He sent a letter to Nick detailing Sharon's sordid past, a past Sharon hadn't gotten around to telling Nick about—she'd had a baby in high school and given it up for adoption. A disbelieving Nicholas confronted Sharon who explained that she was afraid she'd lose Nicholas if he knew the truth. Thankfully, their love was strong enough to see them through this. They made a promise to keep no secrets from each other and planned to elope. Meanwhile, Matt's girlfriend Amy, tired of his scheming and conniving, broke up with him. On the eve of Nicholas and Sharon's wedding, Nick wanted to make love, but Sharon couldn't go through with it, admitting that Matt had violated her. A furious Nicholas tried unsuccessfully to buy a gun, and headed over to Matt's place to settle the score. He arrived just as Sharon's car was pulling away and found Matt face down in a pool of blood. Thinking he was protecting Sharon, Nick was wiping the gun clean of fingerprints just as the

Matt sent this letter and clued Nicholas in to Sharon's past.

Sharon's fairy-tale dreams were turning into a nightmare.

police arrived. He was arrested and put on trial for attempted murder.

Amy, meanwhile, was found wandering the streets of Chicago, and was taken to a shelter where she remained in a catatonic state. A physical exam revealed she had been sexually assaulted. The counselors were unable to get through to their "Jane Doe," but there was a hint of a reaction when they heard "Once in Love with Amy" playing on the radio.

Back in Genoa City, as Matt recovered from his injuries, he remembered that he'd attacked Amy and that she shot him, but he kept the truth to himself so he could see Nicholas Newman pay! Victor hired detective Paul Williams to find the real gunman to clear Nicholas's name. Paul was able to place Amy in town on the night of Matt's shooting. Chasing a lead, Paul, Christine and Victor went to Chicago and found Amy. Relating her own nightmarish experiences, Chris was finally able to get Amy to open up and admit she'd been victimized.

Victor arranged for Amy to be cared for at a private sanitarium in Genoa City. As Nick's trial was nearing its final stage, the jury heard testimony supporting the theory that Nick shot Matt in a jealous rage over Sharon. They convicted him and he was sentenced to 15 years in prison. Slowly making progress, Amy was able to communicate that someone had hurt her. When Victor, Paul and Chris took her to Matt's apartment in an effort to jog her memory, she recalled shooting Matt —but not being attacked. Victor warned Matt they were about to crack the case. Matt decided to pay Amy a visit at the sanitarium and disguised himself as a doctor to gain entry to her room. As he cradled her in his arms and told her how much he loved her, Amy screamed, finally remembering that horrible night! She was able to tell her story to the judge, and the charges against Nicholas were dropped.

Nicholas took the rap for Matt's shooting, thinking he was protecting Sharon, whom he'd seen leaving the scene of the crime.

Below: Nicholas was paying the price for a crime he didn't commit.

BK8271534N
8 01 95
GCPD

Matt knew that Amy was the one who shot him, but he pointed the finger at Nicholas.

It took catatonic Amy a long time before she was able to recall what happened the night Matt was shot. Dr. Hemming helped with her recovery.

Amy's counselors in Chicago saw this ad and called the phone bank Victor had set up. But fearing that those who placed the ad might want to harm Amy, they hung up without identifying themselves. Paul traced the call and headed to Chicago seeking answers.

IF YOU HAVE SEEN THE YOUNG WOMAN IN THIS PHOTO, PLEASE CALL THE 800 NUMBER BELOW. YOUR CALL WILL BE HANDLED WITH THE UTMOST DISCRETION. IT IS EXTREMELY IMPORTANT WE LOCATE HER AS QUICKLY AS POSSIBLE.

Victor Newman vowed to do everything in his power to help Amy after she confessed to shooting Matt. It was her admission that set Nicholas free.

Amy reached out to Chris, herself a victim of rape, and was able to confide in her.

Christine was
with Victor when
he was shot. She
called security,
and summoned
the paramedics
to try to save
Victor's life.

Who Shot Victor?

Someone wanted Victor Newman dead. But who? And what was the motive? Was it Brad Carlton? Brad had been so incensed when Victor informed him his work wasn't up to par that he wrote his resignation letter. Then, to add insult to injury, Victor sent Brad a memo telling him Jack Abbott got the promotion Brad thought should have been his. Brad stormed into Victor's office ready to resign, but Victor beat him to the punch and fired him. Brad was livid. It wasn't his "job performance" that got to Victor; he just couldn't stand the fact that Brad was about to marry his ex-wife, Nikki.

Maybe it was Jill Abbott. She was distraught over Victor meddling in her private affairs and the prospect that she might lose full custody of her son. And that would mean that John Abbott's ex- and maybe soon-to-be wife, Dina, would have a hand in raising little Billy. Just the thought of it made Jill sick! But Victor was concerned about John Abbott's health and told Jill she'd better ease up on his good friend and give in to John's wishes...or else. Victor was her boss, and could make her rue the day she crossed

him! Jill responded by issuing a warning of her own: stay out of her life, or he'd be the one to regret it!

Then there was Mari Jo Mason. Desperate to have a life with Jack Abbott, she would do anything to make it happen. Jack's son, Keemo, who had returned to Vietnam, sent a fax to Victor Newman asking him to protect his father from that "evil woman, Mari Jo." She couldn't bear the thought of Jack finding out about her past, and realized she had to stop Victor from showing the fax to Jack.

In a moment that rocked Genoa City like no other, Victor Newman was gunned down in his own office. Christine was with him, but she only saw the elevator doors close. Victor survived his wounds and was determined to find his would-be assassin. In the end it was revealed Mari Jo had shot Victor out of her obsessive love for Jack. Ironically, it was Mari Jo herself who convinced Victor it was she who held the smoking gun. She came forward after an unnaturally long delay to give Jill an alibi, which would also absolve her. But it didn't work, and her subsequent desperate actions proved to be her undoing.

Brad showed up late to his own wedding, obviously rattled. Nikki left him at the altar and rushed to the hospital to be by Victor's side.

"Wackos"

Wackos often defy definition and/or classification. Some do what they do out of obsessive love or hate or to assuage their tortured souls. Others may be just plain wacky and do what they do for kicks. Many seem perfectly harmless on the outside (it would be inconceivable for them to hurt a mosquito), while inside, they're roiling masses of turmoil waiting to explode. The stories of some of the most memorable, wackiest wackos follow. Their outrageous shenanigans make for good storytelling.

SHAWN GARRETT:
A Grave Error

Shawn Garrett, an obsessed fan of rising young pop singer Lauren Fenmore, was intent on breaking up her marriage to Paul Williams and making her his own. While Lauren sincerely appreciated Shawn's friendship and his interest in her career, he fantasized about having a passionate affair with her. She had no way of knowing that Shawn had bugged the apartment so that he could listen in on Lauren and Paul!

After celebrating the success of one of her concerts in Toronto, Shawn got Lauren drunk on champagne. When she woke up in Shawn's bed, she insisted they forget anything ever happened; she was happily married and they were just friends. If he had a problem with that, then they'd better not see each other anymore. Shawn agreed to Lauren's terms, but continued to obsess. He pushed Lauren toward a solo career, saying it was she who was the star and that Danny was merely riding along on her coattails. He then drugged Danny, causing nearly irreparable damage to his vocal chords. Danny sadly encouraged Lauren to pursue her dream without him.

Lauren was flattered at all the attention showered on her by her biggest fan, Shawn Garrett. She was unaware of the real threat he posed.

Shawn drugged Lauren and buried her alive!

When Lauren uncovered Shawn's bugging device, she told him not to come around anymore. But Shawn threatened to kill Paul unless she obeyed him, and Lauren, convinced that he meant business, saw no way out. She was about to confess everything to Paul when Paul's partner, Andy, was shot. Aware that the bullets were meant for Paul, Lauren decided she had to give in to Shawn's wishes. Under the assumption that Paul was getting on with his life without her, she decided to go to San Francisco with Shawn, where he was planning to launch her on a worldwide concert tour. Paul, Andy and Jazz feared for Lauren's life and followed. In San Francisco, Shawn drugged Lauren, took her to the same cemetery where his mother was buried, placed her in a coffin and lowered it into a makeshift grave. When Paul and Andy spotted Shawn's car at Fisherman's Wharf, they confronted Shawn, who told them Lauren had only three hours to live. The police arrived on the scene and in a bloody shoot-out, Shawn was killed. But he was the only one who knew where Lauren was! A frantic Paul remembered Shawn's dying words—that Lauren would meet the same end as his mother. Rushing to the cemetery, they found a fresh grave right next to Mrs. Garrett's, and Paul and Andy dug up Lauren. She was flown to the hospital in Genoa City where she recovered and resumed her singing career.

San Francisco served as the backdrop for the climax of the Lauren/Shawn Garrett story. It was the first time "The Young and the Restless" went on location outside the Los Angeles area.

Lucky for Lauren, her estranged husband, Paul Williams, and his right-hand man, Andy Richards, figured out Shawn's plot and rescued her.

SVEN:
Hot Stuff in the Freezer

Sven was the masseur at the Genoa City Hotel, where Jill lived. As he was massaging all the kinks and knots out of the tight muscles in her shoulders and neck, Jill mulled over the events of the day. And what a day! In order to win a divorce settlement from John Abbott, she threatened to reveal all about her scandalous affair with his son, Jack. John agreed to all of her terms: 20 percent of Jabot stock, a seat on the board of directors and an executive position in Jabot with an executive salary to match! Sven's hands began to wander: Jill had such a beautiful body—so supple, so sensuous, so seductive. She ordered him to stop. Then he bent down to kiss her. Again Jill ordered him to stop, but Sven persisted. Why was she suddenly acting so high and mighty? She never minded it before. But Jill meant it this time. She called hotel security and they ordered him to leave. To make sure he'd never come to her room again, Jill had Sven fired.

Later, Jill slipped into the shower, preparing for her date with attorney Michael Crawford. Unbeknownst to her, someone had entered her room earlier in the day and was hiding in the closet. The intruder opened the bathroom door and fired three shots at Jill. She crumbled to the floor.

For days, Jill hovered between life and death. When she regained consciousness, she told Carl Williams that Jack Abbott was her assailant. After an exhaustive search, a gun Jack had borrowed from a friend was recovered and tested by ballistics. All evidence pointed to Jack's guilt and he was arrested. Carl then questioned Jill about the details of her divorce settlement, and she told him he'd have to get the information from John Abbott. When John was subpoenaed, Jack confessed to the shooting—even though he didn't do it—because he wasn't about to have his father go through such an ordeal. He then waived his right to a jury trial, which gave the judge discretionary power to impose sentence. Jill admitted to the court that she was wrong to be so vindictive toward Jack, and asked the judge to be lenient in his sentencing. The court obliged.

Jill then carried her penitence to another outrageous degree. She promised Sven she'd help him get his job back as the hotel's masseur, on the condition he spy on

Sven, the master masseur at the Genoa City Hotel, shot Jill Abbott. After she recovered, he locked her in his meat locker freezer when she resisted his advances.

Katherine, whom she was sure had been in collusion with Jack to do her in. Sven, of course, played both sides, and spied on Jill for Katherine. He told Jill he often drank with Jack at Gina's and that Jack had borrowed the gun from Leo, the bartender, a fact which was known only to Jack, Leo and the police. A shocked Jill realized that Sven was her assailant, and here he was again in her hotel room! But she decided to play it cool and agreed to go with Sven to his apartment for a private massage. Jack, by this time, had also come to the realization that Sven was Jill's assailant, and he also made his way to Sven's apartment, with Carl Williams in hot pursuit. Jill, meanwhile, was playing up to Sven, hoping he'd release her, but Sven angrily told her he wasn't going to let her make a fool of him again. He dragged her into a meat locker freezer hidden behind his drapes just as Jack showed up. The two men fought fiercely but Jack fled when the police arrived. After Carl Williams and his men took off after Jack, Sven said good-bye to Jill, turned the freezer on full blast and went on the lam. Luckily, Jack was able to persuade Carl Williams to return with him to Sven's apartment, where they rescued an unconscious Jill from certain death.

DAVID KIMBLE:
The Case of the Restless Sicko

When Nina Chancellor first met David Kimble, he appeared to be a nice, quiet, harmless young man who worked as a private secretary for Nina's mother-in-law, Jill Abbott. As soon as he found out that Nina was worth millions, though, he played up to her and her son, little Phillip, creating a wedge between Nina and her friends Cricket, Chase and Danny. Since Cricket was the closest to Nina and perhaps the most perceptive in terms of what David was up to, she confronted David and faced his ugly temper. He told her that if she continued to interfere, he'd cut her pretty little face to pieces. Moving quickly, David married Nina before her friends could convince her that he wasn't what he seemed. To keep him busy, Nina set him up in business and he began to toy with his secretary, Diane. It wasn't too long before nosy Diane noticed a newspaper clipping on David's desk that showed a picture of Rebecca Harper, an heiress who had been murdered by her husband, Tom, who was also pictured. Funny, she thought, David Kimble was a dead ringer for Tom! And even stranger was that David had given Nina a brooch once owned by the dead heiress! Shortly thereafter, a woman named Vivian, who could tie David to the murder (*if* she could locate the missing brooch) was found electrocuted in her bathtub.

Cricket, Danny and Chase judged David by the company he kept. Here he is with Jill Abbott.

Nina shot David five times, but he survived.
Right: Just your ordinary, everyday kind of couple.

David Kimble Burned Death in Hospital Fir

DAVID KIMBLE

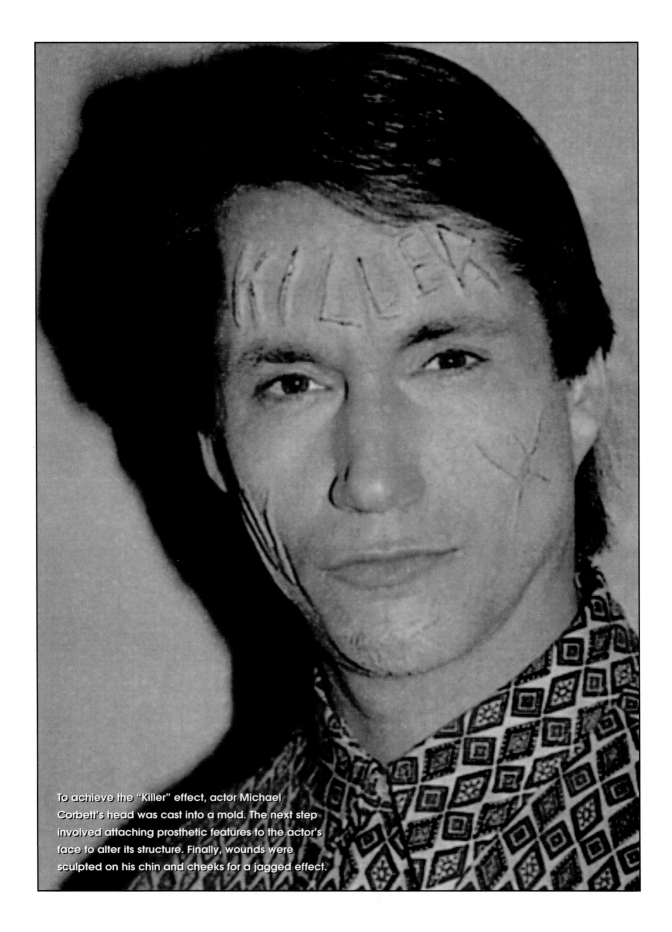

To achieve the "Killer" effect, actor Michael Corbett's head was cast into a mold. The next step involved attaching prosthetic features to the actor's face to alter its structure. Finally, wounds were sculpted on his chin and cheeks for a jagged effect.

When Cricket accompanied Danny to a concert in New Jersey, she found a jeweler who was able to identify the brooch. He said it had been made for one Rebecca Harper, and was commissioned by her husband, Tom (David Kimball). When Nina discovered that David and Diane were planning to kill her, she waited in her apartment for David to return home, and then shot him five times with a newly purchased revolver. She was arrested, and David faked paralysis. But Nina was tried and acquitted, as David schemed and plotted to get even.

David sneaked into the hospital morgue, stole a body, dumped it into his bed and set it on fire. Nina believed her nightmare was finally over. David, however, reunited with Diane and tackled his next quest. He found a plastic surgeon to give him a new face. "Could you make me look like David Hasselhoff?" he asked. To his great chagrin, when Diane removed the bandages they saw that the surgeon had emblazoned the word "Killer" across his forehead! Not to worry—he'd get another disguise. This time he acquired a new chin, a mustache and a head of lighter hair, and he threw in a Southern accent and a new name—Jim Adams. Well on his way to evening the score with Nina, "Jim" married her mother, Flo. Then, at the masquerade ball, he passed himself off as a wolf, and shot Danny, Cricket and Nina. He didn't know the bullets were made of wax. With Paul Williams and the cops hot on his trail, David ducked into a closet, which, unfortunately for him, was really a garbage chute, and he got compacted!

David/Jim Adams told Diane she was the one he really loved. She stood by him in good times and bad and knew him better than anyone else.

David/Jim Adams sweet-talked Flo. He told her it was love at first sight. David knew Flo was the key to Nina's money.

LISA CARLTON:
She's Cagey!

Shelter him. Keep him safe from harm. Cleave only unto him. The vows went something like that, and Lisa took them a little too literally, interpreted them a little differently than most brides do. She wasn't even married to Brad anymore! But she still sheltered him (locked him in a cage); kept him safe from harm (wouldn't let him out); and cleaved only unto him (no other man would do, and no other woman, especially Traci Abbott, would have him, either!).

Brad had married Lisa years ago when she was only sixteen—she was rich, and he saw possibilities. But her father paid him off to get out of her life and Brad thought he'd never see her again. Until, that is, she started calling and worming her way back in. Brad reluctantly agreed to help her settle some financial matters, and she agreed she'd leave him alone after that. Instead, she drugged his glass of wine, undressed him, put him to bed, crawled in with him and took incriminating photos of the two of them. They'd come in handy later. Then she befriended Brad's wife, Traci, and figured it would only be a matter of time before she and Brad would be together again. But Brad wanted Lisa out of his life once and for all, and threatened to kill her if she didn't stop harassing Traci.

Lisa didn't take rejection very well. She'd given him every opportunity to love her, and he didn't respond. So she did what any insane woman in her situation would do: she bought a remote lodge, had a cage built in the living room, hired Rich Little to tape an impersonation of Brad explaining why he'd left town—to be with his true love—and had the tape delivered to Traci. Then, armed with her arsenal of photos, she marched over to Traci's and filled her in: she had been married to Brad, was now having an affair with him and they planned a future together! That done, she kidnapped Brad and locked him in the cell, threatening to burn down the lodge, with him in it, if he toyed with her emotions. She fed him and talked to him for hours. She loved him so.

Lisa hired Rich Little to impersonate Brad on tape. Lauren received one tape explaining why Brad would miss work. Traci's tape explained how he'd run off with his ex-wife, with whom he was madly in love.

Lisa showed Traci pictures of her with Brad and told her they had not only been married in the past, but were planning a future together.

Brad tried to figure out a way to escape.

Jack was looking for Lauren when he stumbled on Lisa. She'd kill him, too, if she had to!

Jack rescued Lauren and Brad.

Brad fell deeper and deeper into despair, but finally realized his only way out was to beat her at her own game—convince her he really *did* love her. So he started to romance her. Falling for it, Lisa planned a romantic evening—wedding dress, tuxedo and all—and joined him in the cage for dinner, then moved to the bedroom. Before they could consummate this newfound "love," Lisa became ill. Brad tried to escape, but got only as far as Lisa's goons at the door and ended up back in the cage.

When Brad got so ill that Lisa feared he might die, she called 911, and was told that Brad should be in the hospital. But Lisa said she'd nurse him back to health herself. When she was filling a prescription, Lauren—who was on a ski trip with Jack—spied Lisa and followed her home. By the time Lisa returned, Brad was unconscious on the floor. Lauren pushed her way in and found Brad, but Lisa pulled a gun on her and shoved her into the cage with Brad. Then she turned on the gas. She flew out the door and bumped into Jack, who was looking for Lauren. When Jack didn't buy her story, Lisa pulled a gun on him. He managed to wrestle it away from her, but she fled while Jack rescued Brad and Lauren from the cage that almost became their coffin!

LEANNA LOVE:
The Vamp Who Hated Men

Would Ashley and Steven Lassiter be enjoying their Hawaiian luau if they knew murderous wacko, Leanna Randolph, wearing a disguise, was among the guests?

Leanna Randolph saw it as her mission to sabotage the marriage of Ashley Abbott and Dr. Steven Lassiter. Leanna, an ex-patient of the good doctor, had escaped from a mental institution and now believed that she was madly in love with him. Before the wedding, Leanna would have fantasies about murdering Ashley. After the wedding, she followed the honeymooners to Hawaii, where she purchased several beautiful leis, over which she sprayed highly toxic poisons, and had them delivered to Ashley. A disguised Leanna attended a luau given for the new bride and groom, and secretly rejoiced when Ashley took ill during the festivities as a result of wearing the poisoned flowers.

Leanna eventually mended her ways and went from being an outrageous lunatic to being just plain wacky, with style, of course. She got involved with Jack Abbott, and, using a pseudonym, penned an unauthorized biography for him entitled *Ruthless: The Victor Newman Story*. Their objective was to destroy Victor Newman. Unbeknownst to either Jack Abbott or Victor, though, Leanna included a chapter called "Victor's Forbidden Love." She had secretly taped Nikki telling all the smarmy details of the Nikki/Victor/Ashley

Jack and Leanna put their heads together. Their objective was to be ruthless in destroying Victor Newman.

Leanna was writing two biographies about Victor Newman: one an unauthorized, scandalous exposé; the other, the authorized version based on fact.

affair—sensational additions that would make her otherwise ordinary book a runaway best-seller. Victor, meanwhile, asked Leanna to write a factual, authorized book on his life. As the author of both books, she managed to flip back and forth between the two, and still land on her feet.

Leanna soon married Victor Newman but refused to sleep with him. She wanted to maintain her virginity. On their wedding night, Leanna slept alone, while Victor shared his bed with his best man, Douglas Austin. Victor found that his off-the-wall psycho-bride had temper tantrums: ranting, raving, screaming, hollering, crying, smashing things against the wall. She liked to cook, boiling pictures of Victor and Jack and others as testimony to her hatred of men. She waged a full-scale "I hate men" campaign on her "Leanna Love" TV show. She wanted children, but she refused to engage in "doing the nasty." Her take-off of Michelle Pfeiffer's sizzling seduction scene from *The Fabulous Baker Boys*, when she sang "You Made Me Love You" was simply that, fabulous.

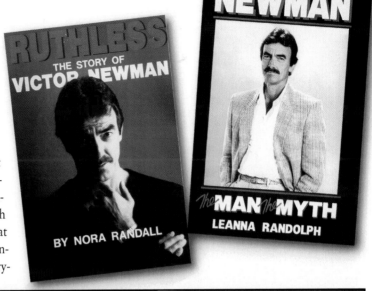

Leanna and Victor married. His objective was to protect Ashley. Hers was "What the heck? Why not? It sounds okay!"

Leanna slithered atop the piano as a birthday gift to Victor Newman.

SHEILA CARTER:
Crossing Over From 53128 to 90036 and Back Again

Lauren, Scott and Sheila, with Paul Williams (left), Lauren's ex-husband and current confidant.

The Sheila Carter/Lauren Fenmore/Scott Grainger story of the nurse from hell who would stop at nothing until she got what she wanted was filled with many memorable moments. From the moment it began, this story kept viewers on the edge of their seats. But to cite one memorable mo-ment would be grievously misleading. For clearly, it is the concept of this story which is "most memorable," and recognition must be given to the man who not only thought up the idea, but who was responsible for the brilliant direction it would take: William J. Bell.

Lauren and Sheila were prepared to fight to the finish over Scott.

Sheila worked in the hospital laboratory to remain close to Scott.

Crossover story lines are nothing new in the soap opera genre. In 1964, for example, "Guiding Light" attorney Mike Bauer was sent from Springfield to Bay City to jump-start "Another World," and in 1970, "Another World" transferred three of its main guns to "Somerset." Then in 1980, "Another World" crossed Iris Carrington into "Texas" territory. In 1968, Dr. Steve Hardy of "General Hospital" went to Llanview for a short visit to "One Life to Live." In more recent years, "Loving" and "All My Children" had their characters hopping from Pine Valley to Corinth. But no one has done crossovers with such aplomb and such success as Bill Bell.

When Sheila dead-ended herself on "The Young and the Restless," she hopped a plane to "The Bold and the Beautiful"—flying from Genoa City (53128) to Los Angeles (90036). The mix worked both in terms of story and ratings. The two shows have crossed over numerous times, shuttling other characters such as Brad (Genoa City), Eric (Los Angeles) and Lauren (Genoa City) back and forth. Lauren, like Sheila, is today a permanent resident of Los Angeles. Some of the plot points that over the next few years made Sheila so unredeemable, requiring her exile from Genoa City:

Sheila stole Lauren's husband, Dr. Scott Grainger, seduced him and became pregnant with his child. Lauren, too, was carrying Scott's child but was so upset over his infidelity that she left without telling him, against ex-husband Paul's advice. Sheila moved in with Scott and miscarried, but she wore a pregnancy pad to hold on to him. After Lauren gave birth, Sheila switched Lauren's baby with one she got from the black market. She now had Scott's biological baby, Scotty, and Lauren had a brokered baby, Dylan, who later fell ill and died. Molly Carter, Sheila's mother, discovered the truth, but suffered a stroke before she could disclose Sheila's deception to Lauren. Sheila then kidnapped Lauren and was about to murder her when a fire broke out in the Carter farmhouse, thwarting her plans. It was thought that Sheila perished in the flames; instead she escaped to Los Angeles and got a job as nursemaid to Eric Forrester's small son on "The Bold and the Beautiful." Eric Forrester, of course, was a longtime friend of Lauren Fenmore and all the elements for the crossover story were in place.

Lauren and Scott argued frequently over the long hours he spent doing his research in the hospital lab.

Sheila helped Scott in every way she could—in his research and in his personal life.

After moving in with Scott, Sheila had the advantage of his expert advice regarding her pregnancy.

Scott frequently visited Lauren and liked to play with her little boy, Dylan, who later died.

Sheila was a good mother to her "son," Scotty.

Sheila's mother, Molly, confronted
her about the baby-switching caper.

A fire engulfed the Carter farmhouse where Molly lived and where Sheila presumably perished in the flames. The
special effects department at CBS tended to the fire in the studio, ensuring everyone's real-life safety.

After Dylan's death, Lauren
obtained custody of her own son,
little Scotty, and became close to
Sheila's mother.

Phyllis was determined to do whatever she could to keep the home fire burning in Danny's heart.

Danny and Phyllis observed a milestone at the christening of little Daniel.

Baptismal Certificate

Daniel Romalotti, Jr.
child of Daniel Romalotti, Sr., and Phyllis Summers Romalotti
born on the 9th day of July 1994
was baptized as recorded in the baptismal register of
St. Elmo's Catholic Church
on the 20th day of March 19 95
by Father Francis McCarthy
Godparents Paul Williams and Christine Blair

PHYLLIS ROMALOTTI:
Fire and Ice

She was the new girl in town, this redheaded firecracker and "ballsy broad," Phyllis Romalotti. Her mission was to reclaim her husband, rock star Danny Romalotti, and have the three of them—Phyllis, Danny and precious little baby Daniel—live together as a family. So obsessed was she with accomplishing this mission that she was prepared to run roughshod over anyone who would dare get in the way.

Phyllis knew she could handle Danny's sister, Gina. And if Danny's dad, Rex, gave her trouble, then she'd just introduce herself, push her baby in his face, complain about how Danny abandoned them and plead for him to intercede. She'd tell him to teach his son about honor, responsibility, duty and family. When Rex went and got himself killed before he could do any real good, Phyllis showed up at the wake, dressed to the nines in black. She introduced herself to the assembled family and friends as Danny's wife and the mother of his son.

Now, if *Christine* gave her any trouble....But why should she? She was now engaged to Paul, except that Danny kept throwing it in Phyllis's face that he still loved Christine! So if need be, take more drastic steps to get Christine permanently out of the way.

Yep, she had it all figured out, this hell-on-wheels, dangerous, neurotic, impetuous woman! She'd soon have Danny in her bed! She did it once, she could do it again. But what is it they say about the best laid plans of mice and men? Oh, God, she had to work harder! Danny was unimpressed with everything she threw his way, and she had to change her tactics, be more cunning, more coy, shrewder, even reasonable. She proposed a four-month trial marriage to Danny: if it didn't work out, he'd be free to go. She'd wear her most seductive little teddies, pry him with good food and wine, tease him, teach little Daniel to call him "Daddy"!

Nothing seemed to work and Danny still wanted a divorce. Then she hit on it! She'd get professional help, see a marriage counselor.

"Get with it," the counselor said. "Relax. Get a new life."

So she decided to get a new boyfriend, a guy named Peter Garrett. Instead of getting jealous, Danny approved of Peter. Phyllis decided to go on a little vacation with Peter and little Daniel, making it impossible for Danny to see his son. Then she locked Danny out of the apartment, curtailing his freedom to see his boy, and had him arrested when he broke down the door! When the court ruled on a hearing, Phyllis threw everything into the hopper, and Dr. Timothy Reid was assigned as a marriage counselor to both parties. Poor, nerdy, unsuspecting Dr. Reid! Phyllis steamrolled him right into her bed, and taped the entire tryst. See you in court! At first, Dr. Reid wrote a report recommending the continuation of the marriage, but in the end, he privately confessed to the judge about his misconduct, and the judge reversed himself. Divorce granted!

Family, friends and godparents assembled for an amicable pose shortly after the christening.

When Danny and Phyllis reviewed the photographs taken at the christening, Danny noted how upset Phyllis became when she saw one of Christine holding Daniel. He quickly pocketed the photo.

Unsuspecting Dr. Timothy Reid fell victim to Phyllis's scheming.

Phyllis and Danny got into one of their disagreements over the care of little Daniel. Why did she leave the baby with Peter Garrett, whom they hardly knew?

Issues and Enlightenment

Soap operas are, first and foremost, an entertainment medium. But they're also fertile ground for telling a different kind of story—a story that can enlighten and inform. Throughout the years, "The Young and the Restless" has been recognized and applauded for telling stories that address important social issues, conveying valuable information to the audience. The nature of the medium allows these painstakingly researched stories to unfold in real time. Some of the most memorable stories ever told on "The Young and the Restless" have been these types of stories: groundbreaking, compelling stories to which viewers can relate, about characters with whom they can identify. They resonate at a societal, even a personal level for viewers, making viewers think, helping them cope.

Breast Cancer

Jennifer Brooks's battle with breast cancer and her resulting mastectomy were the first time this disease was dealt with on the soaps. Estranged from her husband, Stuart, and in Chicago to see her old flame Bruce Henderson, Jennifer discovered a lump in her breast. Bruce urged her to have a biopsy. When the tumor was found to be malignant, she refused to consent to the surgery that could save her life. Jennifer returned to Genoa City where her four distressed daughters finally managed to convince her to go through with the mastectomy. The story dealt realistically and compassionately with all of the pertinent issues faced by Jennifer, including her fear that her life would be irreparably changed; her anger and loss of self-esteem; and her withdrawal from male companionship. She underwent counseling and started to rebuild her life, and Stuart was there for her and helped her to understand that she was no less a woman because she had lost a breast.

Other characters on "The Young and the Restless" have also faced the fear of breast cancer. It was fortunately only a scare for Mary Williams and Katherine Chancellor, but the importance of early detection and mammography was conveyed to the audience through their stories.

Jennifer's husband, Stuart, and the rest of her family helped her cope with breast cancer and regain her self-esteem.

Eating Disorders

Staking out new ground in the mid-70s, "The Young and the Restless" told the story of young Traci Abbott, a teenager willing to do just about anything to control her weight problem. Traci had many insecurities and was deeply worried that she would lose Danny Romalotti to beautiful and slender Lauren Fenmore. This fear propelled her to shed more than a few pounds, as fast as possible. A battle with bulimia and an addiction to diet pills almost cost Traci her life. With the support of her family, who helped her realize that beauty lies within, Traci was able to get her life back on track. She talked about her problem to the audience at Danny's concert, saying that there were more sensible ways to go about losing weight, and that the "ideal" body image many strive for is a fallacy. Traci's struggle resonated with many a teenager and young women.

Traci Abbott was the first soap opera character to struggle with the eating disorder bulimia.

The Homeless

After Jack Abbott was found guilty of shooting Jill, he was sentenced to a work release program. This provided the perfect opportunity for "The Young and the Restless" to feature the plight of the homeless. Assigned to the Grant Avenue Shelter, Jack's first job was to serve the hungry in a soup kitchen.

The shelter helped the homeless of Genoa City find reprieve from the streets. As the story progressed, viewers became aware not only of the importance of the shelter to its patrons, but also of the difficulty such facilities have staying afloat because of ever-tightening purse strings. Touched by the shelter's good work—and smitten with its director—Jack Abbott anonymously donated a large sum of money to ensure it would remain open and accessible to the people who so desperately depended on it.

Jack Abbott learned what life was like for the homeless when he served soup in a Genoa City shelter.

Jack fell in love with Ellen, who ran the Grant Avenue Shelter, but she was drawn to his father, John. Eventually, she left Genoa City for a job in Washington.

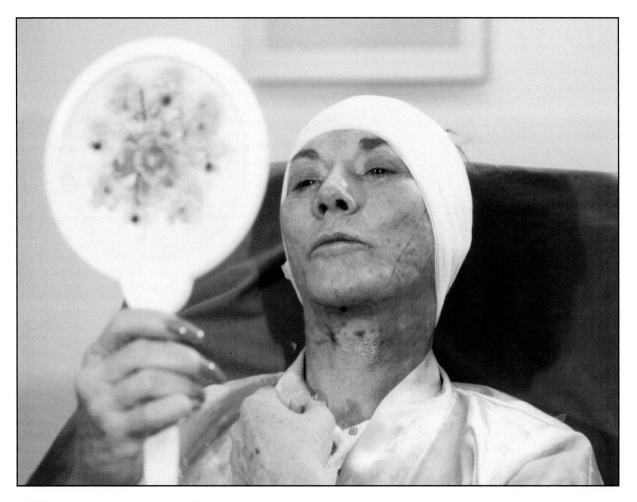

Cosmetic Surgery

On March 26, 1984, viewers of "The Young and the Restless" witnessed actual face-lift surgery, something never before seen on daytime television. Actress Jeanne Cooper had been on the show for over 10 years, and wanted to have cosmetic surgery. The producers decided to incorporate this into the show, for if Jeanne Cooper had a face-lift, then her character, Katherine Chancellor, would have to have one, too! The cameras followed her into the operating room, and it was a truly memorable moment when, two days later, as the bandages were re-moved, Jeanne Cooper, along with all of America, saw the results of the surgery. In episodes that preceded and followed this moment, the show, in almost documentary-like fashion, enlightened viewers about all facets of cosmetic surgery, including how to find the right doctor; how to identify quack doctors; how to know if a face-lift is right for you; and, of course, the operation, the recovery and the psychological effects of such surgery.

Viewers witnessed actress Jeanne Cooper's reaction to the removal of her bandages as Katherine Chancellor's story was being told. The episodes garnered huge ratings as viewers were glued to their television screens following this riveting and unusual story.

Black-Market Babies

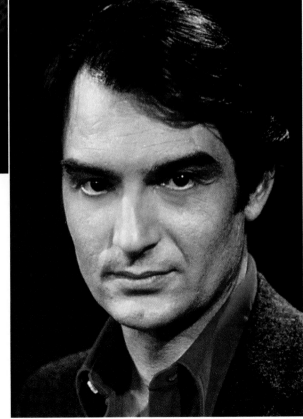

The Young and the Restless" explored the underground world of black-market babies when a pregnant Nina Webster, seeking shelter from the streets, was taken in by baby broker Rose DeVille. Rose made a business of arranging to sell babies to couples who'd been turned down by adoption agencies. When Nina had a change of heart and decided she wanted to keep her baby, Rose lied and said the baby was dead, and then completed the transaction with the adoptive parents. Cricket helped Nina discover the truth about Rose and her illegal operation.

The story concerned not only Nina's plight, but the struggles of other unwed teen mothers who, while fighting to get out from under a life of despair, tragically fell prey to the baby-selling ring.

Rose DeVille and her partner in crime, Vince Holliday, ran a black-market baby-selling ring, preying on mothers-to-be and young unwed mothers. They eluded the police and are still at large.

Drinking and Driving

Young Phillip Chancellor would occasionally down a couple of drinks when he got nervous; it calmed him down and helped him overcome his shyness. But he was sure he could handle it, and believed it was just a social thing. Nobody knew that Phillip had been spiking his own drinks when he was at a party one night. When he drove Cricket home, he ran a stop sign and plowed into another car. Afraid Phillip would go to jail for DWI, Cricket switched seats with him before the police arrived on the scene and took the blame for the accident. As a result, she almost lost her job, until Phillip confessed and vowed to kick the habit. It was a struggle, but he finally got his life together.

He eventually had it all: a new wife, Nina, a young son he adored and a terrific life to look forward to as heir to the Chancellor fortune. But he still had a drinking problem. Phillip went to Alcoholics Anonymous, but he was different from the other people there. After all, what were a few drinks among friends? That's what he was thinking when he and his coworkers celebrated a business deal by cracking open a bottle of champagne. After downing his share, Phillip headed home, excited to tell Nina the good news. He should have known better than to get behind the wheel in his condition. This time, Phillip Chancellor never made it home. He crashed his car, holding on just long enough to tell Nina and baby Phillip how much he loved them.

The tragedy of Phillip's death rang all too true—a young life snuffed out in its prime in a drunk-driving accident. It was one of the saddest moments ever shown on "The Young and the Restless." The show was honored by Mothers Against Drunk Driving for this realistic portrayal.

Phillip's friend Cricket tried for years to get him to quit drinking. He made a fatal mistake by getting behind the wheel of his car after celebrating at the office.

Teen Model Pleads Guilty To Reckless Driving

Phillip's fatal accident wasn't the first time he drove under the influence. Once before, Cricket took the rap for him by switching seats before the police arrived. The bad publicity from that accident almost cost Cricket her modeling job at Jabot.

John Abbott married Jessica, and then nobly stepped aside so that Jessica could give Cricket the family life for which she so desperately longed. Jessica later wrote to John, asking him to ensure that she'd die with dignity, and professing her unfailing, eternal love for him.

AIDS

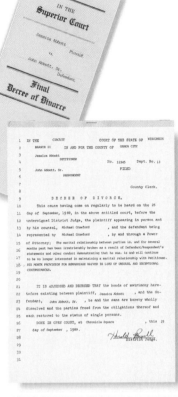

Several compelling stories explored the issue of acquired immunodeficiency syndrome (AIDS), providing information to viewers about how the disease is transmitted; how the risk can be diminished; and the physical, mental, emotional and psychological ramifications associated with the disease. "The Young and the Restless" first dealt with this issue in depth with the plight of Cricket's mother, Jessica. It was as much a story about AIDS as it was about tolerance, unconditional love and sacrifice.

When she found out she was dying of AIDS, Jessica reunited with her daughter, whom she had given up when she was very young. Jessica wanted, in some small way, to try to make up for all those missing years. John Abbott fell in love with Jessica, and she with him. She initially kept her illness a secret, and she could hardly believe it when John still wanted to marry her after finding out the truth. Immediately after the ceremony, the newlyweds informed their family of her illness and John's children supported his decision to stay with his wife. The writers dealt sensitively with the issue of living with someone with AIDS.

In a supreme sacrifice, John gave up the woman he deeply loved so that she could live out her final dream—to be a family with Cricket and Cricket's father—with whom she'd recently been reunited.

The Grainger family reunited shortly
before Jessica died of AIDS.

Jessica managed to give Cricket
the greatest gift she could—a family.
Pictured here in happier times,
Cricket and her mother tearfully
read the Twenty-third Psalm and
sang "You and Me Against the
World" moments before Jessica
passed away, content that she'd
lived her dream.

CPR

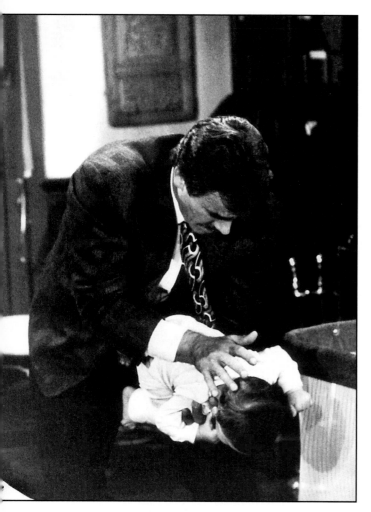

Victor Newman saved the life of his young son, Nicholas, as Eric Braeden demonstrated the proper technique for infant CPR.

When young Victoria Newman was searching for a lost dime, she noticed something was very wrong with her baby brother, Nicholas. Acting quickly, Victor saved his son's life by performing infant CPR. Nikki was so grateful that Jim Grainger, whom she was dating, had to question whether she could ever truly give her heart to any man other than Victor.

In real life, Joy Townsend, Safety Specialist with the American Red Cross, spent time on the set teaching Eric Braeden (Victor) the proper technique for infant CPR. Choking is one of the leading causes of death for children aged 6–18 months, and the episode was used to help the ARC launch its campaign on Infant and Child CPR.

In a related story, Nikki discovered young Victoria face down in the Newman swimming pool. Jack rescued her and administered CPR, saving her life. The very afternoon this episode aired, a viewer found her own child lifeless in the family swimming pool. She used CPR to save her son's life. The next morning she telephoned the show's creator, William Bell, to express her gratitude.

The information presented on the show helped her and other viewers understand the procedure and taught them how to act in an emergency situation. This time, the blending of entertainment and information on "The Young and the Restless" literally saved a life.

Nikki was forever indebted to Jack for saving young Victoria from drowning.

Date Rape

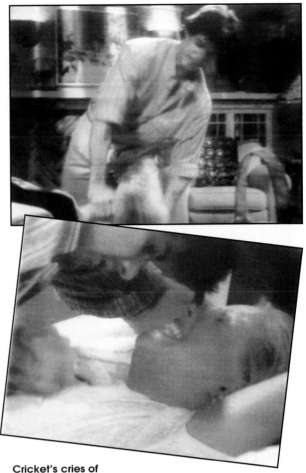

Twenty-year-old Jabot model Cricket Blair succumbed to the charms of clean-cut, seemingly mild-mannered Derek Stuart, becoming the victim of a date rape in her own apartment. Nina took her to the hospital for medical attention. Cricket had the courage to press charges, and the story followed her through the ordeal of Derek's trial, where she fought accusations that she'd "asked for it," and wrestled with her own questions of self-doubt. Derek ultimately got his comeuppance and was convicted. While awaiting sentencing, he eluded authorities and went to see Cricket again. When the police and Cricket's father and brother stormed the penthouse, Derek, with nowhere else to turn, dove through the window to his death.

This story was handled in a realistic, informative and sensitive manner. Cricket was the typical victim: innocent, inexperienced, unable to see the warning signs. And Derek was a likely attacker because he'd earned Cricket's trust. The rehearsals and choreography of the scene took nine hours to ensure that everything was handled just right. When the filming of the scene was over, actress Lauralee Bell had the bruises to show for it; makeup wasn't needed to show the physical scars from her attack. And Cricket's emotional scars took a long time to heal, as the story unfolded true to life.

This story was played out during the summer months when viewership among younger people is greatest. The Center for Population Options recognized the show's efforts and presented "The Young and the Restless" with its prestigious Nancy Susan Reynolds Award for Outstanding Daytime Drama. The show received numerous letters and telephone calls from young women who identified with Cricket's ordeal and, as a result, were better able to cope with the aftermath of their own attacks.

This story was not the first time the issue of rape was tackled on "The Young and the Restless." In 1974, it was the first soap opera to present an extended rape story line when George Curtis (played by Anthony Geary) attacked Chris Brooks. This groundbreaking story exposed viewers to the myriad legal, emotional and psychological ramifications of this crime of violence.

Cricket's cries of "No!" "Don't!" "I don't want this!" fell on deaf ears as Derek overpowered her.

No one would ever suspect that handsome Derek Stuart was capable of rape.

Nathan was prepared to help Drucilla overcome the hurdles she faced to become a responsible and enlightened citizen.

Illiteracy

As illiteracy was emerging as a serious issue in the United States, "The Young and the Restless" featured the problem in some hard-hitting stories. In 1986, the show was honored with the Film Advisory Board's Award of Excellence—the first time this award had ever been presented to a daytime serial—for its story about reformed mobster Kong, who realized he didn't have a chance with Amy, the woman he loved, unless he made something of his life. Ashamed that he was illiterate, Kong accepted Amy's offer to teach him to read, with the provision that he stay away from his corrupt friends.

In a more recent story, streetwise runaway Drucilla Barber, the niece of Abbott maid Mamie Johnson, returned to Genoa City and continued her pickpocketing ways. But Nathan Hastings took sympathy on her when he accidentally found out she couldn't read. He managed to help her turn her world around by turning her on to reading and writing. Experts trained in teaching adults to read were brought in to advise the show and ensure the authenticity of Drucilla's lessons.

Both stories portrayed the humiliation, frustration and triumph that accompany an adult's earnest effort to learn to read.

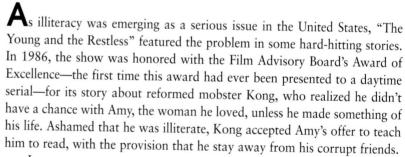

Nathan was able to pass along the gift of literacy to Drucilla, just as Amy had done for him.

Teenage Pregnancy/ Crack Babies

In her position as a Legal Aid attorney, Cricket Romalotti counseled many needy clients, including Julie Sanderson, a pregnant teenage drug addict. Julie went to see Cricket when she lost her job: she said it was because she was pregnant; her boss said it was her drug habit. Cricket and Danny tried to educate Julie about the effects of continued drug use on her and her baby. The message finally hit home when they convinced Julie to accompany them to the hospital to witness crack babies fighting for their lives. Viewers got a glimpse of this tragic world as Julie struggled through withdrawal, was tempted to get back into drugs, and lost her baby. She eventually was able to kick the habit and reenroll in school.

"The Young and the Restless" addressed the issue of teen pregnancy many times over the years, from many different perspectives. In 1986, the show was honored by Los Angeles Mayor Tom Bradley and El Nido Services, a United Way Agency, for educating the public about this problem and helping social service organizations provide effective assistance to their clients.

Danny was concerned that Cricket might be putting her own life in danger by involving herself in Julie's world. Danny's concerns were warranted as Julie's drug dealer thought Cricket was in the way.

A trip to the hospital to see the tiny, helpless babies born addicted to crack was enough to convince Julie to enter a drug rehab center.

Julie struggled through withdrawal, and Cricket was right by her side to see her through it.

Alcoholism...

My name is Katherine and I'm an alcoholic." It was an electric, emotionally charged moment when Katherine Chancellor admitted her problem and was finally able to muster the courage to attend an AA meeting. The suspense built up for some time: her son Brock, husband Phillip and companion Jill urged her to take that all-important first step. But it took Katherine's fear of losing Phillip to Jill to force her to take action. She was impressed that there were other affluent people at the meeting, each reciting the 12 Steps. When it was time for the new members to speak, Katherine's chair was empty! She later returned and spoke her turn. Brock was there and said he'd never been prouder of his mother.

Katherine's battle continued—with her drinking literally creating the situation that would lead her to deliberately steer her car over a cliff, killing Phillip. Brock helped her get back on the wagon, and by the mid-1980s, Katherine seemed to be winning the fight.

While drunk, Katherine Chancellor signed her divorce papers. Her alcoholism drove her husband Phillip into Jill's arms. Katherine finally took a monumental step when she admitted she was an alcoholic, but she spent years falling off the wagon and climbing back on again.

...and Addiction

While Katherine Chancellor used her drinking to deaden her emotions, Nikki Newman Abbott was trying to mask the physical pain she was suffering as the result of a riding accident. Unable to face the back surgery that would either relieve her pain or possibly leave her paralyzed, she found herself depending more and more on painkillers and alcohol. Nikki's decline became the centerpiece of the clash of the titans—husband Jack and ex-husband Victor—each of whom felt they knew the best way to help Nikki cope. Eventually, Nikki had surgery and went through rehab, regaining control of her life. What viewers witnessed was a riveting story showing the emotional roller coaster of a woman trying to cope with chronic pain...and eventually conquering it.

Nikki was flirting with disaster by combining pain killers and alcohol. Anything was better than the risky surgery recommended by her doctor.

Nikki's fall from a horse caused her to suffer lingering, excruciating back pain.

Victoria and Ryan's sexual encounter was too much for the young teen to handle.

Safe Sex

In the late 1970s, "The Young and the Restless" showed the fallout of care-free sex in a story involving Paul Williams and Nikki Reed that dealt with a sexually transmitted disease. More recently, lonely 16-year-old Victoria Newman got in way over her head with her boyfriend (later husband) Ryan McNeil. After she and Ryan made love, Victoria confessed to her stepmother Ashley that she didn't know if he had used a condom. Frank discussion on the matter provided important information to viewers: just one unprotected sexual encounter puts both partners in danger of contracting sexually transmitted diseases, including AIDS. Victoria was emotionally unprepared for an intimate relationship. She had to submit to a pregnancy test, as well as a series of HIV tests, and got a lecture from her doctor on the dangers of casual sex and on how to practice safe sex. Victoria learned a hard lesson. It was a timely story with an important message.

Ashley got Victoria to confide in her, and had a good, long talk with her stepdaughter about the importance of abstinence until she was emotionally mature enough to handle an intimate relationship.

Seniors Rights

Feisty seniors Margaret and Miles rallied their neighbors and fought to get the much-needed repairs made to their apartment building.

The Young and the Restless" has often made it a point to present youth-oriented storylines during the summer months, but in 1993, the show broke with tradition to explore an issue relating to television's—and, unfortunately, society's—much-neglected elderly population. The golden-agers were being exploited by their landlord and sought help from Cricket Romalotti's Legal Aid office. The seniors staged a rent strike and demanded repairs be made to their building. Their request was ignored by the slumlord, who sold the building to a developer, giving the tenants only six weeks' notice to vacate. Attempts at delaying the sale were futile. But word that the Rainbow Gardens were housed in a building commissioned by Civil War hero Garfield Dandridge Chancellor led Cricket on a quest to have the building declared a historic landmark.

The cause brought Margaret and Miles together, and they were married, with newfound friends Cricket and Paul by their side.

Cricket Romalotti was pleased to accept a job working at the law firm of her mentor, attorney Michael Baldwin.

Michael stepped over the line with Cricket when he made sexual advances on the job.

Sexual Harassment

In one of the most challenging issue-oriented storylines ever tackled on "The Young and the Restless," Cricket Romalotti found herself the victim of sexual harassment by her new boss, attorney Michael Baldwin. Michael promised Cricket she'd have a stellar career at the law firm and he would help her up the corporate ladder, if she would "cooperate" with him. He assured her that her professional performance would only be enhanced by their having a strong personal relationship. His advances strengthened Cricket's resolve to seek justice and she filed a lawsuit against Michael. This despite warnings from other partners that such an action would likely hurt her career and damage her husband Danny's reputation. Michael tried to turn the tables by saying it was he who had to rebuff Cricket's advances, but in the end, Cricket's story proved true, and Michael was found guilty. He lost his job, and was censured by the Wisconsin State Supreme Court.

This story was written to help viewers recognize the signs of sexual harassment and to teach someone on the receiving end of such treatment how to handle the situation. It won "The Young and the Restless" a nomination as Outstanding Daytime Drama from the Center for Population Options.

Cricket pressed charges against Michael Baldwin, but the partners in the law firm didn't believe her accusations.

Michael Baldwin got Hilary, a former employee, to marry him—fast. He thought his status as a happy newly-wed would be a good cover for the charges against him.

Supreme Court of Wisconsin

BOARD OF ATTORNEYS PROFESSIONAL RESPONSIBILITY
P. O. BOX 6158
ELKHORN, WISCONSIN 53121-3383
TELEPHONE: (608) 555-2965

CHRISTINE ROMALOTTI, Petitioner
vs.
MICHAEL BALDWIN, Respondent

This matter comes before us for review of an Order entered by a Panel of the Board of Attorneys Professional Responsibility Committee.

The Panel's Order finds the Respondent, Michael Baldwin, guilty of sexual harassment, concluding his conduct consitituted a violation of the Code of Professional Conduct for Attorneys, and recommends formally censuring him for that conduct.

The tape recording of the Respondent's conversation with Mrs. Romalotti while the two were in Los Angeles clearly reflects sexual harassment of a most insidious nature; making it a condition of employment that the woman surrender to the sexual demands of superior. The recording also corroborates the testimony of two other Panel witnesses — Hilary Baldwin and the young woman Bridget — who came forward to give evidence that was undoubtedly embarrassing to themselves, but critical to the prosecution of this case.

All three women — Christine Romalotti, Hilary Baldwin, and Bridget — are to be commended for their courage in presenting this evidence. It is the Court's strong hope that others who find themselves similarly harassed will also come forward to seek justice.

As for the ruling of this Court: we find that Mr. Baldwin unquestionably made Mrs. Romalotti's continued employment conditional upon her agreeing to engage in sexual relations with him, and, in fact, unequivocally fired her when she refused. No more telling evidence of sexual harassment could have been introduced. Any suggestion of problems in Mrs. Romalotti's marriage is not deemed pertinent to the fundamental issue of her having been sexually harassed. Accordingly, it is the judgment of this Court that the finding and conclusions of the Panel be affirmed. We uphold the formal censure of Michael Baldwin.

Danny supported Cricket in her attempt to trap Michael Baldwin. They staged a breakup and, when Cricket went on a business trip to Los Angeles with Michael, she recorded him making a play for her. The tape proved to be Baldwin's downfall.

Sexual Harassment Issue Before Board of Attorneys

Michael Baldwin

Michael Baldwin was censured for his sexual harassment of Cricket.

MOST MEMORABLE
Roxies and Remotes

Producing a soap opera five days a week, fifty-two weeks a year is a Herculean task for everyone involved: the cast, writers, producers, directors, production designers, set decorators, musicians, costume designers, wardrobe, makeup, hair, casting—everyone. Multiply that effort by 10 and you'd come close to what's required when it comes to putting together roxies and remotes. What is a roxy? Roxies are the bigger-than-life productions, the cast of thousands-type scenes that viewers see when some element of production—the sets, the costumes, the music or a combination—is raised to a much-higher-than-usual level. They're the types of productions that would make any big-screen moviemaker proud.

Then there are the remotes, when cast and crew venture outside the comfortable confines of the studio into the great outdoors—as well as the great indoors. The very first scene in the very first episode of "The Young and the Restless" was shot on location in California's San Fernando Valley as viewers saw Brad Eliot roll into Genoa City. Since then, the remotes have gotten bigger and better. Whether just around the corner or halfway around the world, these "on location" shoots make for interesting experiences and beautiful and authentic presentations.

"The Young and the Restless" does not enter into roxies and remotes lightly. There's no such thing as a roxy just for the sake of a roxy, or a remote just for the sake of a remote. They're both done for the sake of story. And many a story has culminated with one of these big productions. The lavish sets and lush surroundings have made for some truly memorable moments for all the inhabitants of Genoa City—those in front of as well as those behind the scenes.

Beautiful Leslie Brooks, the celebrated piano virtuoso, was accompanied by Lance Prentiss as she was warmly received by her many European fans.

The Gala Ball

Never in her wildest dreams had Leslie Brooks imagined that her virtuosity at the piano, as exhibited at the European Music Critics Gala Concert, would win her such plaudits and honors! Wined and dined by royalty, the ultimate accolade was the invitation to attend the event of the year—the royal wedding of Charles, Prince of Wales and Lady Diana Spencer. Leslie was accompanied by her proud father, newspaper publisher Stuart Brooks, and his beloved Liz, radiant in red; family friend Katherine Chancellor; and the love of her life, Lance Prentiss. Leslie, herself striking in black, felt secure that the future would obliterate all the bitterness she felt toward her sister Lorie. Until, that is, Lorie, ravishingly beautiful in a provocative blue strapless gown, cast the entire assemblage, including Lance, under her spell, with Leslie once again in her sister's shadow.

Lance and Leslie enjoyed a waltz...and each other.

The Gala Ball marked something of a turning point in the history of "The Young and the Restless." At the time, it was the biggest roxy ever staged. Production designer Bill Hultstrom felt that since the story being told was about an entrance, a grand entranceway should grace the sound stage. So the show's first two-story, in-studio set was built to achieve the splendor necessary to accompany Leslie's—and Lorie's—moment. One of the biggest challenges turned out to be the ballroom floor! It had to be marble—what else for such an opulent grand ballroom? But the original plan to paint the back of linoleum to simulate marble would have made camera movement extremely difficult. They instead decided to paint the studio floor. The floor was so large, though, that it took days to complete and dictated how and when the show could be shot!

Lorie Brooks appeared unexpectedly at the Ball with famed French filmmaker, Jean Paul Vauban.

Katherine Chancellor attended the Ball with the intention of later exploring the European continent for a competent plastic surgeon.

Stuart Brooks and his wife, Liz Foster Brooks, posed proudly with Leslie.

Music With a Message

Danny and Lauren toured together when his career was just getting off the ground. A poster promoted one of their concerts.

Music has always been a critical element distinguishing "The Young and the Restless" from other daytime serials. Some of the most memorable musical moments have been the big-production rock concerts Danny Romalotti staged for his fans in Genoa City and on the road. At the same time, fans of the show have thrilled to the music of real-life rocker Michael Damian, who has written many original songs specifically for the show. It's not by accident that these concerts could pass for MTV's hottest new videos. For the most recent concert scenes, the show hired the very same technicians that set things up when the big names perform in Los Angeles. The look of Danny's concerts owes much to lighting director Ray Thompson, who utilizes sophisticated computer technology to synchronize the lighting to the music, and director Mike Denney, a drummer himself, who knows exactly what he's looking for when the concerts are staged. The songs are recorded in advance, and concerts are painstakingly taped, shot by shot—with the editing process resulting in the look of a real-life concert. What viewers might not realize is that 15 minutes of a Danny Romalotti concert may have taken eight hours or more to shoot...and over a month to plan!

Amidst all the fun and excitement, the music usually delivered a message tied into the stories being told at the time: teen pregnancy, date rape, the hungry and homeless and other social issues.

Michael Damian does much of his own choreography for Danny's concerts. Musicians in Danny's band have included "Young and Restless" music coordinator Jack Alloco on bass.

BENEFIT CONCERT
for THE HUNGRY & HOMELESS
FRIDAY JUNE 17, 1988

NO PASSES ACCEPTED THIS PERFORMANCE

It was usually music with a message when Danny Romalotti gave a concert.

Danny called on former singing partner Lauren Fenmore to help him get the message out that "It's OK to say no."

"The Young and The Restless" show-cased the singing talents of Michael Damian, Tracy Bregman Recht, Beth Maitland and Patty Weaver. Genoa City residents heard Danny, Lauren, Traci and Gina.

Danny was so moved by the loneliness and despair of young teen mothers that he planned a special concert in Genoa City and invited Amy to help increase awareness of the problem.

Danny and Traci sang "Be Good to You," a song Michael Damian wrote especially for the show.

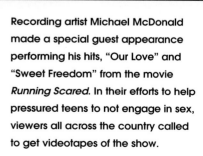

Recording artist Michael McDonald made a special guest appearance performing his hits, "Our Love" and "Sweet Freedom" from the movie *Running Scared*. In their efforts to help pressured teens to not engage in sex, viewers all across the country called to get videotapes of the show.

Danny's concerts started small, but have grown more elaborate as the years have passed. They used to be produced in one of the two CBS studios where "The Young and the Restless" tapes, but because the productions have grown to include 200-300 extras and sophisticated special effects, the concerts are now produced on another CBS sound stage that can better accommodate them.

ENTERTAINMENT SECTION

Romalotti Wows 'Em Again
Hometown Star Better Than Ever

Katherine and Rex were King and Queen
(of Hearts) of the ball.

The Masquerade Ball

The Masquerade Ball, charity event of the year in Genoa City, was the "roxiest" roxy of all—the most elaborate production ever to be staged by "The Young and the Restless." The lavish production tested the mettle of the entire ensemble. The idea was to create a striking venue for the culmination of the David Kimble story. According to his plan, David, disguised in a costume to match Danny's, would kill Nina, Cricket and Danny, and literally get away with murder. But the bullets in his gun had been replaced with blanks, and his scheme failed. David was pursued by the police, fell into a trash compactor and was crushed to death.

"Big Bertha" was so big and heavy that it required a special truck to transport it from Warner Bros., and a special hoist to get it into place in the studio. This chandelier appeared in many old movies from Hollywood's heyday.

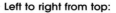

Left to right from top:

Cricket dances with her husband Danny…or is it David?

Ryan and Victoria came to the Ball dressed as Romeo and Juliet. They were, in Victoria's mind, truly tragic lovers because Victor disapproved of his daughter's relationship with the young man.

Brad just learned that he was about to become a father. How would Zorro take such news from Mae West?

When Olivia had to work late, Nathan and Dru wound up together.

Ashley as Scheherazade probably has unending stories to tell about her relationship with Victor.

Jill talked her stepson Jack into escorting her to the Ball, but Prince Charming Jack had Nikki on his mind.

Little Bo Peep may have lost her sheep, but Nina found a friend in handsome toreador John Silva. Silva's costume was rented—tattered and torn. The costume designers made repairs and worked their magic to transform it into a real showpiece.

An unlikely couple: Captain Intrepid and Marie Antoinette. Paul couldn't dance the night away with Lauren because he was called into action in hot pursuit of David Kimble.

The Ball also provided the perfect opportunity for viewers to glimpse some moments in the relationships of other prominent Genoa City residents: Jill spelled trouble for Katherine and Rex; Leanna stepped between Jill and John; Jack pined over Nikki who was in rehab...or was she?

It took about five weeks to prepare for the Ball. A huge two-story set built in the studio featured the pièce de résistance of all set decorations: "Big Bertha." This chandelier was rented from Warner Bros. Studios and had a 50-year motion picture pedigree. The set took 24 hours to set up and many of the cast and crew spent up to three days at the studio, sleeping in their dressing rooms or rented trailers in CBS's parking lot.

More than anything, the Masquerade Ball was "Young and Restless" costume designer Greg York's shining moment. He designed numerous original costumes and embellished dozens of rented ones, turning those that were sometimes rough and tattered into rich, lavish showpieces. Costumes for every character were carefully chosen to reflect individual personalities, and the results couldn't have been more befitting: Victor as a Roman conqueror; Paul as a comic book superhero; Katherine as the Queen of Hearts; Leanna Love as Cupid; David as the wolf; and Esther as (surprise!) a French maid. Everything about the Ball was spectacular: bigger, splashier, more memorable than ever before!

That's Kay's son, Brock, as Teddy Roosevelt with Flo as Little Orphan Annie...who wouldn't go anywhere without Sandy.

What costume could be more fitting for Genoa City's Victor Newman than that of a Roman conqueror?

Costume designer Greg York (with Jennifer Johns of wardrobe) is surrounded by his original creations for the Ball.

If only John would lavish as much attention on Jill as "Cleopatra's guards" did!

Death in Paradise

Rick Daros endeared himself to Nikki by trudging through a blinding blizzard to the Genoa City Hospital, cradling a feverish Baby Victoria in his arms. But he was also certifiably mad—the killer of his first wife Melissa who had allegedly drowned in a swimming pool accident in Hawaii. Insanely jealous of Nikki's every move, Daros lured her to St. Croix. Once there, he created a scene in a souvenir shop after Nikki took too long to select a pair of cuff links for Victor Newman.

Luckily for Victor, who was on their trail along with private investigators Paul Williams and Andy Richards, the shopkeeper easily recalled the commotion Daros created and directed the would-be rescuers to the village of Easterly where Daros and Nikki were living. But the road to the village was washed out and Victor had to hire the captain of a schooner who was willing to risk taking them out in the choppy waters. Vowing that Nikki would meet the same end as Melissa and die in a scuba diving accident, Daros held her at gunpoint, ordered her to assemble her gear and then let the air out of her tank. Just as Victor, Paul and Andy arrived to rescue her, Nikki broke away from Daros and was plucked from the water by Paul and Andy. Daros severely wounded Victor in the groin with a speargun, before he disappeared from sight into the ocean.

At this time in its history (1984), "The Young and the Restless" relied primarily on the Los Angeles region when its stories called for exotic locations. In this case, Palos Verdes in Southern California substituted for exotic St. Croix.

Rick and Nikki admired the Caribbean—the site of Nikki's first—and possibly last—dive!

Rick Daros terrified Nikki.

Paul, Victor and Andy arrived on the beach, desperately hoping it wasn't too late to rescue Nikki.

A Murder Mystery Far From Home

The alluring, much younger Cassandra Rawlins dreamt of the tremendous wealth she stood to inherit once her ailing husband George passed on.

Carl Williams declared that his son's "suicide" was an admission of Paul's guilt, thereby causing the police to close the case. Mary Williams never believed her son would take his own life and vowed she would not rest until her son's murderer was caught.

For more than a year, the George Rawlins murder mystery kept viewers of "The Young and the Restless" in suspense as they tried to guess who killed the sterile, vengeful, terminally ill tycoon. There were more twists and turns to this whodunit than a giant roller coaster at the world's most elaborate amusement park. Even the actors were kept in the dark as to who the real killer might be.

Rawlins's charismatic, gorgeous young wife, Cassandra, was already hopelessly smitten with handsome supersleuth Paul Williams, who could keep neither his hands nor his eyes off her. On the pretext of hiring Paul to manage his business affairs, Rawlins soon uncovered the couple's incendiary love affair, and he put into motion a master plan to frame Paul for his "murder." With the help of his father, police detective Carl Williams, Paul was forced to go undercover to save his own hide by faking his death when it became apparent that his beloved was involved in the ultimate betrayal. For Cassandra's lover, Adrian Hunter, was not only the real thief of hearts, but Rawlins' actual killer.

As the denouement to this mystery drew near, the actors went on location to the sumptuous warmth of Bermuda, where Paul and Carl plagued both Cassandra and Adrian with mysterious voices and visions from beyond the grave. In a stellar moment after Cassandra set herself up as a pawn by marrying Adrian, she realized that her own death by Adrian's hands was imminent. Using dry ice to activate the murder weapon, Adrian set his own diabolical scheme in motion only to have it backfire. The exquisite irony was that some months later, Cassandra did die. She was hit by a truck!

Searching for a location with an international flavor, producers chose Bermuda for their first "really big" remote for "The Young and the Restless," taking them out of the country far away from their L.A. studio. One of the challenges in doing such a production is trying to ensure that everything needed for the sets would be easily accessible. What that meant for the set decorators was that they did a lot of packing—26 steamer trunks full of necessities accompanied them to the exotic location! To add authenticity, the show hired many locals as extras. A typical workday lasted 16 to 18 hours, but it was worth it; Y&R fans got a real treat when they saw the story unfold in this tropical paradise.

Once Paul was set up as the fall guy for the murder of George Rawlins, Cassandra and Adrian stole away to Bermuda, unaware that Paul and his father were in hot pursuit.

No love was more consuming, more passionate than the love Cassandra Rawlins and Paul Williams felt for each other.

Adrian and Cassandra were carefree lovers in Bermuda: sharing a private tête-à-tête, frolicking in the sun and caressing on the beach.

Once the production team arrived, they set up shop in the
Stouffer hotel. A contingent of staffers scouted out locations
in St. Thomas in advance of the scheduled tape dates.

The Bougainvillea Remote

Recently, St. Thomas, Virgin Islands, provided the backdrop for memorable twists and turns in the lives of some of Genoa City's most prominent residents. While Jack Abbott was contemplating life with long-lost love Luan, mysterious Mari Jo Mason tried everything to get him to marry her. Despite all their frolic and fun in the sun, by the end of the trip Jack knew his heart would always belong to Luan. Meanwhile, Ashley Abbott Bladeson was hoping to get her marriage to Blade back on track—maybe a romantic holiday was the answer. For her, the trip was the beginning of a terrible nightmare. She'd soon learn that Blade's evil twin brother, Rick, locked Blade up and kept him on the island while he assumed Blade's identity and took Blade's place in her life back in Genoa City.

Even though Jack had planned to make the trip to romantic St. Thomas with Luan, Mari Jo hoped she and Jack would be together.

Ashley and Blade thought a vacation together might restore happiness to their failing marriage. Their problems were only beginning!

Brad and Mari Jo shared some small talk, but Brad wondered why she was there.

Brad lent a sympathetic shoulder to Ashley, who suspected Mari Jo had come to St. Thomas for a secret rendezvous with Ashley's husband, Blade.

Neither Blade nor Mari Jo thought Rick would go so far as to assume his brother's identity.

Outdoor scenes like this one presented unique challenges, not the least of which was getting the cooperation of Mother Nature!

Nearly 30 members of the cast and crew traveled to the Caribbean. The remote's nickname, "Bougainvillea," refers to the colorful silk flowering vines that were brought in from the States and intertwined to fill in the open latticework in the portico where scenes were being shot. The process took hours for the set decorators to complete! This attention to detail, combined with the natural splendor of St. Thomas, resulted in some of the most beautiful and memorable sequences ever seen on "The Young and the Restless."

Cameraman Rege Becker sat precariously close to the edge to get the shot he needed. The proximity of the helicopter to the boat made this scene extremely dangerous to shoot.

That wild and crazy family at
"The Young and the Restless."

MOST MEMORABLE
Lighter Moments

Producing an hour-long episode of "The Young and the Restless" every day is hard work, but it doesn't always look that way. Sometimes the actors welcome a change of pace and appear on other shows. The CBS Soapbreak specials have given cast members a chance to step out of character and be themselves. On the network's prime-time "Diagnosis Murder," the actors were able to to play themselves in the story. And famous fans have occasionally stopped by the studio and landed themselves a guest appearance. On the set and off, the "Young and Restless" family finds time to share a smile or a laugh, about the expected...and more often the unexpected. All these things add up to lighter moments that have been captured by the camera.

"The Young and the Restless" is noted for its casting of young, beautiful actors, and who could argue? Shemar Moore, Tonya Lee Williams, Diana Barton, J. Eddie Peck and Michelle Stafford prove the critics right.

The CBS Soapbreak specials highlight the real-life adventures of the network's soap opera stars. Host Kristoff St. John spent some time with John McCook, Carol Burnett and Peter Bergman. Maybe Carol will visit Genoa City sometime soon, or help Eric Forrester with his next fashion show?!

CBS Soapbreak Specials/ "Diagnosis Murder"

A few of the show's hunks ham it up for the CBS Soapbreak special (Shemar Moore, Kristoff St. John, Don Diamont and J. Eddie Peck).

"The Young and the Restless" added a little twist to the crossover story concept when its stars guested on an episode of "Diagnosis Murder" titled "Death in the Daytime." Series star Dick Van Dyke welcomed them to the show, which was shot on Y&R's soundstages at CBS Television City in Hollywood.

Cameos

Above: In 1991, Geraldo Rivera played himself, asking Traci Abbott if she'd consider being a guest on his talk show.

Below: In August 1983, then Edmonton Oiler star Wayne Gretzky made a cameo appearance on "The Young and the Restless" as an underworld cohort of scheming kingpin Tony DiSalvo. His character's name? "Wayne." Here he poses with Jon St. Elwood, Joseph Taylor, Doug Davidson and Steven Ford.

Football players Tony Dorsett and Flipper Anderson (right) can be counted among the show's biggest fans. Each has made a cameo appearance.

Behind-the-Scenes Moments

Former president Gerald Ford visited the set in 1987. His son, Steven (second from left), played detective Andy Richards.

Jon St. Elwood, Nathan Purdee, Stephanie Williams and
Steven Ford in disguise.

Were they boning up on their lines? Actually, it's just
Heather Tom and Michael Damian (or is it Michael
Corbett?) killing some time between takes.

What does Amy (Stephanie E. Williams) want for
Christmas? Maybe Santa Claus Jazz Jackson (Jon St.
Elwood) can find out!

When Jeanne Cooper found out that the members of Circus Vargas, the last remaining traveling tent circus in the United States, stopped whatever they were doing to watch "The Young and the Restless" every day, she invited them to the set. Doug Davidson tried some acrobatics with his new friends.

Just hold on tight and hope for the best! Ed Scott and his wife, Melody, share a light moment before she goes for a ride on the Newman Ranch.

Who shot Jill? That's what the cast and crew wanted to know. They've rounded up the usual suspects.

Animals on the set always present a challenge. Is this horse trying to tell J. Eddie Peck something? The horse can't begin to compare with the snake in the shower...or the freeze-dried tarantulas...

When Dru got pregnant, she wasn't sure if the baby was Neil's or Malcolm's. Kristoff St. John and Victoria Rowell cracked up when they saw the prop doll, "Baby Shemar," complete with eyebrows and telltale goatee.

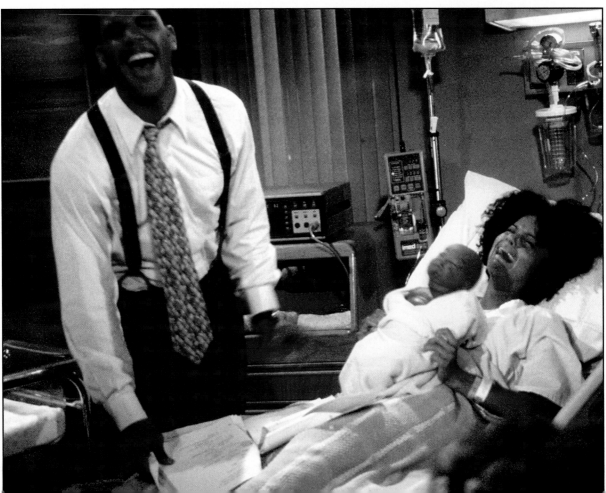

Joshua Morrow and Melody Thomas Scott waiting for their cue. Does Nikki have slippers to coordinate with every outfit?

Peter Bergman and Melody Thomas Scott found it's sometimes hard to keep a straight face.

Six of the beautiful leading ladies of "The Young and the Restless" join veteran actor Robert Colbert to celebrate the show's 10th anniversary. (Left to right) Deanna Robbins (Cindy Lake), Colbert (Stuart Brooks), Deborah Adair (Jill Abbott), Meg Bennett (Julia Newman), Eileen Davidson (Ashley Abbott), Stephanie Williams (Amy Lewis) and Patty Weaver (Gina Roma).

Celebrations and Milestones

"The Young and the Restless" premiered on March 26, 1973. Since that time, they have marked many a happy occasion with simple little get-togethers and the most extravagant of parties. There have been so many milestones along the way, signifying the monumental moments in the show's history and pointing the way toward successes yet to be. Some of the most memorable of all of these memorable moments have been preserved so that everyone can share in the celebrations.

In a celebration of the show's 10th anniversary on March 26, 1983, original cast member Julianna McCarthy was toasted by several of the series' leading men. (Top, left to right) Terry Lester (Jack Abbott), Jay Kerr (Brian Forbes), Chris Holder (Kevin Bancroft), Steven Ford (Andy Richards). (Seated, left to right) John Denos (Joe Blair) and Michael Damian (Danny Romalotti).

Anniversaries/Honors

Happy Anniversary! Not many television programs can boast taping 4,000 episodes—that's over fifteen years and counting! "The Young and the Restless" decided to mark the occasion by serving up an enormous cake!

Columbia Pictures Television hosted a tribute to Bill Bell on February 10, 1992, in honor of his 35th anniversary in daytime television. At the time, conservative estimates placed the worldwide daily viewing of Bell's two shows at 40 million.

Bill and Lee Phillip Bell were honored by CBS in March 1990 for 20 consecutive years on the network—17 years for "The Young and the Restless," and three years for "The Bold and The Beautiful." They accepted leather-bound original first scripts for both shows from Lucy Johnson, Vice President of Daytime Television for CBS, in the executive dining room of the studios in Los Angeles.

Bill Bell and his wife, Emmy award-winning broadcast journalist Lee Phillip Bell, cocreated "The Young and the Restless." Mr. Bell has been head writer since it first aired in 1973, longer than anyone else in the history of daytime television drama.

Bill Bell was treated to a special video roast/toast with the help of special guest host Carol Channing, stars from his past and network and studio executives. The event was held at Chasen's California Room in Los Angeles. Here, daughter Lauralee, executive producer Ed Scott, wife Lee, Jeanne Cooper and Michael Damian congratulate Bell on his accomplishments.

Write me a story! Maybe that's what these stars are whispering in Bill Bell's ear. And he has! For a total of over 10,000 daytime TV episodes airing continuously and without repetition since 1956!

In 1993, Michael Damian and his character, Danny Romalotti, starred in Andrew Lloyd Webber's musical *Joseph and the Amazing Technicolor Dreamcoat*. Damian's run as "Joseph" began at Los Angeles's famed Pantages Theater, allowing him to continue with "The Young and the Restless." When the musical headed to Broadway, Damian (and Danny), were wished good luck and temporarily written out of Y&R. The show was a big success.

"The Young and the Restless" has celebrated many milestones over the years, but few as memorable as the taping of episode No. 5,000. The party was held right at the studio, and when the celebration ended, they got started on the next 5,000!

Melody Thomas Scott and Doug Davidson had the honors of presenting show creators Bill and Lee Bell with a proclamation by Los Angeles Mayor Tom Bradley, who declared October 29, 1992, "Young and Restless Day."

In a moment that will be long remembered, CBS dedicated and renamed Studio 43—home to "The Young and the Restless" since the first episode—in honor of William J. Bell. The red carpet was rolled out for the event as Lucy Johnson did the unveiling.

On March 26, 1993, "The Young and the Restless" celebrated its 20th anniversary in posh style at the Four Seasons Hotel in Los Angeles. David Hasselhoff, who played Dr. Snapper Foster, served as master of ceremonies and helped cut the TV…er…cake!

As part of the 20th anniversary celebration, Bill Bell paid tribute to senior cast member Jeanne Cooper, who started on the show in 1973. The incredible cast, teamed with outstanding writers, producers, directors and behind-the-scenes talent, have made for an incredible on-air run!

Bill Bell celebrated with Coordinating Producer Nancy Bradley Wiard, who has been connected with the show since its inception. They're flanked by Peter Tortorici (then president of the CBS Entertainment Division) and Scott Siegler (then president of Columbia Pictures Television).

August 20, 1993, marked a memorable moment for actress Jeanne Cooper when she received her star on the famous Hollywood Walk of Fame. She was honored for a stellar career that has spanned over 40 years of motion picture and television work, including a nice long stint on "The Young and the Restless." Her family, sons Corbin and Colin Bernsen, daughter Caren and grandsons Westin and Oliver, were on hand to help Jeanne celebrate.

In 1994, Producer David Shaughnessy, Bill Bell, Ed Scott and Nancy Bradley Wiard attended a double celebration: six years at number one and the first "Young and the Restless" prime-time special.

On March 12, 1996, the show marked yet another milestone: eight years and running as the top-rated daytime soap on television! Executive Producer Ed Scott had the honor of addressing the guests.

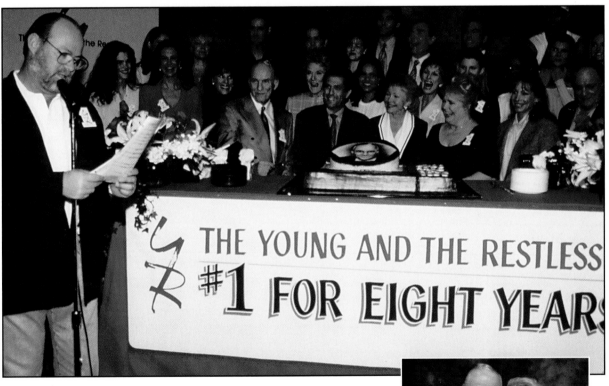

On that same day, Bill Bell celebrated another personal milestone—his birthday.

Emmys

In 1992, the National Academy of Television Arts and Sciences presented the writers of "The Young and the Restless" with the Daytime Emmy Award for Outstanding Writing in a Daytime Drama. Pictured are Kay Alden (with her husband Vernon Nelson), Jerry Birn, Bill Bell and John F. Smith (with his wife Norma).

In 1993, "The Young and the Restless" won its fifth Emmy Award for Outstanding Daytime Drama. The show also took home the statue in 1975, 1983, 1985 and 1986.

Melody Thomas Scott and Eric Braeden had the honor of hosting the 23rd Annual Daytime Emmy Awards in May 1996. The show aired immediately following the third "Young and the Restless" prime-time special.

1996 was a banner year for the show, with numerous Emmy nominations, a testimony to the collaboration—in front of and behind the cameras—that makes the show such a success!

In 1992, the National Academy of Television Arts and Sciences presented William J. Bell with The Governor's Lifetime Achievement Award. His peers recognize him as master storyteller and genius. He is the driving force behind the success of the show; the patriarch of an incredible, memorable, "Young and Restless" family!

Memorable Moments: Cast List

ASHLEY ABBOTT	Eileen Davidson	STUART BROOKS	Robert Colbert
	Brenda Epperson	BRAD CARLTON	Don Diamont
	Shari Shattuck	COLLEEN CARLTON	Natalie/Victoria
BILLY FOSTER ABBOTT	Shane Silver		McCormick
	Blake Pontello	LISA CARLTON	Lynne Harbaugh
	Josh M. Rose	SHEILA CARTER	Kimberlin Brown
JACK ABBOTT	Terry Lester	PHILLIP CHANCELLOR II	Donnelly Rhodes
	Peter Bergman	PHILLIP CHANCELLOR III	Thom Bierdz
JILL FOSTER ABBOTT	Brenda Dickson	PHILLIP CHANCELLOR IV	Charles/Kenneth
	Deborah Adair		Gravino
	Jess Walton		Scott/Shaun Markley
JOHN ABBOTT	Jerry Douglas		Courtland Mead
LUAN VOLIEN ABBOTT	Elizabeth Sung	MATT CLARK	Eddie Cibrian
NIKKI NEWMAN ABBOTT	Melody Thomas Scott	BRANDON COLLINS	Paul Walker
DETECTIVE BOB ADAMS	David Combs	DORIS COLLINS	Karen Hansel
JED ANDREWS	Tom Selleck	STEVE CONNELLY	Greg Wrangler
ALANA ANTHONY	Amy Gibson	TRACI ABBOTT CONNELLY	Beth Maitland
JOSEPH ANTHONY	Logan Ramsey	JACK CURTIS	Anthony Herrera
DOUGLAS AUSTIN	Michael Evans	JOANN CURTIS	Kay Heberle
MICHAEL BALDWIN	Christian LeBlanc	REVEREND DANIELS	Warren Stanhope
KEVIN BANCROFT	Christopher Holder	RICK DAROS	Randy Holland
LYNNE BASSETT	Laura Bryan Birn	BRENT DAVIS	Bert Kramer
KAREN BECKER	Brandi Tucker	ROSE DEVILLE	Darlene Conley
NANCY BECKER	Cathy Carricaburu	TONY DISALVO	Joseph Taylor
RON BECKER	Dick DeCoit	MARGARET DUGAN	Maxine Stuart
ALEX "BLADE" BLADESON	Michael Tylo	MILES DUGAN	Parley Baer
RICK BLADESON	Michael Tylo	BRAD ELIOT	Tom Hallick
JOE BLAIR	John Denos	CAROLE ROBBINS EVANS	Christopher Templeton
CHRIS BROOKS	Trish Stewart	SKIP EVANS	Todd Curtis
JENNIFER BROOKS	Dorothy Green	SKYLAR EVANS	Emma/Mallory Brooks
LAURALEE "LORIE" BROOKS	Jaime Lyn Bauer	DYLAN FENMORE	Gregory/Nathan
LESLIE BROOKS	Janice Lynde		Griesbach
	Victoria Mallory	LAUREN FENMORE	Tracey Bregman-Recht
LIZ FOSTER BROOKS	Julianna McCarthy	NEIL FENMORE	James Storm
PEGGY BROOKS	Pamela Peters Solow	GREG FOSTER	James Houghton
	Patricia Everly		Wings Hauser

Memorable Moments: Cast List

DR. SNAPPER FOSTER	William Grey Espy	AMY LEWIS	Stephanie E. Williams
	David Hasselhoff	FRANK LEWIS	Brock Peters
WILLIAM FOSTER, SR.	Charles Gray	APRIL STEVENS LYNCH	Cynthia Jordan
SHAWN GARRETT	Grant Cramer	DR. ROBERT LYNCH	Terrence McNally
ERIC GARRISON	Brian Matthews	MALCOLM	Shemar Moore
JESSICA ABBOTT GRAINGER	Rebecca Street	JOANNA MANNING	Susan Seaforth Hayes
DR. JIM GRAINGER	John Phillip Law	MARGE	Jeanne Cooper
	John O'Hurley	MARI JO MASON	Diana Barton
SCOTT GRAINGER	Peter Barton	NINA McNEIL	Tricia Cast
SCOTTY GRAINGER	Hannah/Jessica Gist	RYAN McNEIL	Scott Reeves
REVEREND GREER	Christopher St. John	DINA ABBOTT MERGERON	Marla Adams
ROBERT HASKELL	Ryan MacDonald	MARC MERGERON	Frank M. Benard
SHIRLEY HASKELL	Ruth Silveira	CORA MILLER	Dorothy McGuire
NATHAN (KONG) HASTINGS	Nathan Purdee	MINISTERS	William Knight
	Randy Brooks		Rev. Bob Bock
	Adam Lazzare-White		Earl Boen
NATHAN (NATE) HASTINGS	Shantel/Shenice Buford		Bobbie Holtzman
	Bryant Jones	KEESHA MONROE	Jennifer Gatti
DR. OLIVIA BARBER HASTINGS	Tonya Lee Williams		Wanda Acuna
DR. DEBORAH HEMMING	Anneliza Scott	MOREY	Morey Amsterdam
VINCE HOLLIDAY	Alex Rebar	JULIA NEWMAN	Meg Bennett
COLE HOWARD	J. Eddie Peck	NICHOLAS NEWMAN	Marco/Stefan Flores
EVE HOWARD	Margaret Mason		John Nelson-Alden
VICTORIA NEWMAN HOWARD	Ashley Nicole Millan		Joshua Morrow
	Heather Tom	SHARON COLLINS NEWMAN	Sharon Case
ADRIAN HUNTER	Mark Derwin	VICTOR NEWMAN	Eric Braeden
JAZZ JACKSON	Jon St. Elwood	PARAMEDIC	David Fabrizio
TYRONE JACKSON	Phil Morris	NORMAN PETERSON	Mark Haining
MAMIE JOHNSON	Marguerite Ray	POLICE OFFICERS	Lazarus Jackson
	Veronica Redd-Forrest		Steven J. Saucedo
JUDGE	James Harper	LANCE PRENTISS	John McCook
KEEMO	Phillip Moon		Dennis Cole
DAVID KIMBLE	Michael Corbett	LUCAS PRENTISS	Tom Ligon
CINDY LAKE	DeAnna Robbins	VANESSA PRENTISS	K.T. Stevens
HILARY LANCASTER	Kelly Garrison	CLINT RADISON	James Michael Gregary
DR. STEVEN LASSITER	Rod Arrants	FELIPE RAMIREZ	Victor Mohica

LEANNA RANDOLPH	Barbara Crampton	DEREK THURSTON	Joe LaDue
CASSANDRA RAWLINS	Nina Arveson	ESTHER VALENTINE	Kate Linder
GEORGE RAWLINS	Jonathan Farwell	KATE VALENTINE	Darla/Sandra Greer
DR. CASEY REED	Roberta Leighton	JEAN PAUL VAUBAN	Michael Carvin
DR. TIMOTHY REID	Aaron Lustig	MAI VOLIEN	Marianne Rees
BROCK REYNOLDS	Beau Kayzer	WALLY	Joey Sciacca
ANDY RICHARDS	Steven Ford	FLO WEBSTER	Sharon Farrell
MIGUEL RODRIGUEZ	Anthony Pena	LINDSEY WELLS	Lauren Koslow
GINA ROMA	Patty Weaver	CALVIN WESLEY	Erwin Fuller
DANNY ROMALOTTI	Michael Damian	DIANE WESTIN	Devon Pierce
DANIEL ROMALOTTI JR.	Desiree/Hanna Whelan	SALENA WILEY	Fay Hauser
PHYLLIS ROMALOTTI	Michelle Stafford	CARL WILLIAMS	Brett Hadley
CHUCKIE ROULLAND	Marc Bentley	CHRISTINE BLAIR WILLIAMS	Lauralee Bell
PIERRE ROULLAND	Robert Clary	MARY WILLIAMS	Carolyn Conwell
SALLY McGUIRE ROULLAND	Lee Crawford	PATTY WILLIAMS	Lilibet Stern
JULIE SANDERSON	Kari Kupcinet		Andrea Evans Massey
MICHAEL SCOTT	Nicholas Benedict	PAUL WILLIAMS	Doug Davidson
MITCHELL SHERMAN	William Wintersole	AMY WILSON	Julianne Morris
JOHN SILVA	John Castellanos	CLIFF WILSON	David Cowgill
KATHERINE CHANCELLOR STERLING		HOPE WILSON	Signy Coleman
	Jeanne Cooper	DRUCILLA BARBER WINTERS	Victoria Rowell
REX STERLING	Quinn Redeker	ELLEN WINTERS	Jennifer Karr
DEREK STUART	Ken Olandt	LILY WINTERS	Elyse/Erin Williams
TIM SULLIVAN	Scott Palmer	NEIL WINTERS	Kristoff St. John
SVEN	Lee Nichol		

Memorable Moments: Photo Credits

All photos, unless otherwise noted, courtesy of Columbia Pictures Television, Bell Dramatic Serial, Co. and CBS.

Special thanks to CBS photographers Monty Brinton, Tony Esparza, Cliff Lipson and Geraldine Overton. Photographer credits, where available, are as follows:

16-17: Cliff Lipson

24: bottom, Randy Tepper

24-25: Randy Tepper

26-27: all, Randy Tepper

29: Cliff Lipson

30-31: all, Cliff Lipson

37: bottom left and middle, Monty Brinton

38: top right and bottom, Monty Brinton

40: Michael Yarish

41: bottom left, Michael Yarish; top right, Monty Brinton

42: top left, Michael Yarish

43: bottom right, Monty Brinton

44: Cliff Lipson

45: all, Cliff Lipson

67: bottom left, Richard Cartwright

70: top right, Monty Brinton

71: all, Michael Yarish

72: bottom, Monty Brinton

73: bottom, Monty Brinton

74: Cliff Lipson

93: top left, Monty Brinton

94: bottom, Cliff Lipson

95: bottom, Monty Brinton

104-105: all, Monty Brinton

106: Monty Brinton

110: Gene Arias

111: Cliff Lipson

112: top, Cliff Lipson

115: all, Michael Yarish

139: top right, Monty Brinton

143: top right, Monty Brinton

147: top right, Richard Cartwright

148: top right, Richard Cartwright

150: right, Michael Yarish

151: all, Monty Brinton

152: top left and right, Michael Yarish

154-155: Richard Cartwright

161: bottom, Monty Brinton

162: top left and right, Cliff Lipson

171: top, Richard Cartwright

172: all, Monty Brinton

173: all, Cliff Lipson

174-175: Monty Brinton

176: all, Monty Brinton

178-179: Monty Brinton

187: top, Tony Esparza; bottom, Geraldine Overton

189: Monty Brinton

191: bottom, Michael Yarish

192: top left, Monty Brinton

194: Cliff Lipson

195: all, Cliff Lipson

196: all, Monty Brinton

197: top, Monty Brinton

198: bottom left, Monty Brinton

199: all, Monty Brinton

200: Cliff Lipson

201: Monty Brinton

202-203: courtesy Steve Schapiro

204: bottom, Geraldine Overton

213: bottom, courtesy Steve Schapiro

217: middle, courtesy Barry Wittman

218: top right and bottom right, Cliff Lipson

222: Murry Neitlich

225: Jerry Fitzgerald

232: top, Monty Brinton

237: top, Monty Brinton; bottom, Cliff Lipson

261: bottom right, Monty Brinton

265: top, Monty Brinton; bottom, Ron Tom

268: bottom left, courtesy Barry Wittman; bottom right, Geraldine Overton

270: bottom, Monty Brinton; bottom, Ron Tom

271: all, Cliff Lipson

275: middle right, Crissy Ogden

277: top right, courtesy Craig Schwartz/Jay Thompson; bottom, Monty Brinton

281: middle and bottom, Tony Esparza

282: top right, courtesy John Paschal/Celebrity Photo

Front cover: Randy Tepper, Monty Brinton, Geraldine Overton
Back cover: all, Monty Brinton

"Y&R" logo designed by Sandy DeVore